MACMILLAN/McGRAW-HILL

Math

Leveled Problem Solving

Grade 2

Macmillan
McGraw-Hill

To the Teacher

Leveled Problem Solving offers differentiated instruction for all students. Each page provides leveled word problems to be used in conjunction with *Macmillan/McGraw-Hill Math*. The problems correlate to each lesson's objectives and ensure that students can read, solve, and explain their thinking about math problems.

The word problems are written at three levels of difficulty. **Basic** problems (questions 1 and 2) are presented in easy-to-follow language for students who need help with basic skills. **On Level** problems (questions 3 and 4) match the language of the actual lesson for students who have the required skills. **Challenge** problems (questions 5 and 6) offer an opportunity for enrichment for those students who excel.

Leveled Problem Solving serves as a math literacy tool to help all students become successful problem solvers.

Contents

Numbers

Count. Write the number.

1. How many ? _____

2. How many ? _____

Count. Write the number.

3. How many ✏ does Sherry have? _____

4. How many does Brian have? _____

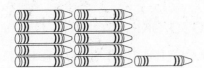
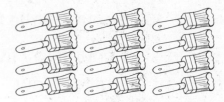

Write the numbers.

5. Anil goes on a trip. He packs his shirts.

How many shirts does Anil pack? _____ shirts

How many dark shirts does he pack? _____ dark shirts

6. Paula and Kerry go to the beach.
Paula found starfish.
Kerry found shells.

How many things did both girls find? _____ things

Who found more? _____

Number Patterns

 Skip-count. Write the numbers.

1. How many balloons?

_____   _____

_____ balloons

2. How many wheels?

_____   _____

_____ wheels

 Skip-count. Write the numbers.

3. Emma skip-counts by fives to count minutes. How does she count?

5, 10, ____, 20, ____

_____ minutes in all

4. Rosa skip-counts by twos to count the shoes in her closet. How does she count?

2, 4, ____, ____, ____

_____ shoes in all

 Skip-count. Tell how you got your answer.

5. There are 4 sets of twins at Josh's school. How can you skip-count to find the number of children that are twins?

____, ____, ____, ____

I can skip-count by _____.

6. 10 cards fit on each page. Ellen has 4 pages of cards. How can she skip-count to find how many cards?

____, ____, ____, ____

She can skip-count by ____.

Understand Addition and Subtraction

Add or subtract. Draw a picture to help.

1. 10 ducks are in the water.
2 swim away.
How many ducks are left?

_____ ducks

2. 3 fish are in a bowl.
8 fish are in a tank.
How many fish in all?

_____ fish

Add or subtract.

3. 3 robins are on the bush.
6 robins are on the grass.
How many robins are there in all?

_____ robins

4. 11 birds sit on a fence.
5 fly away.
How many birds are left on the fence?

_____ birds

Add or subtract. Write a number sentence.

5. Ana has 6 fish.
Laura has 2 kittens.
How many pets do they have in all?

_____ ◯ _____ ◯ _____

_____ pets

6. José catches 12 crabs in the net.
He lets 8 of the crabs go.
How many crabs does José keep?

_____ ◯ _____ ◯ _____

_____ crabs

Problem Solving Skill:
Reading for Math

Mary goes to the lake.
She sees an alligator swimming.
She sees dragonflies above the water.
2 swans are standing in the grass.

 **Use the illustration to solve items 1–6.**

1. How many swans are at the lake?

_____ swans

2. 4 more swans come. Now how many swans are there? _____ swans

 Solve.

3. Skip-count by twos. How many dragonflies do you see? Write the numbers.

_____

_____ dragonflies

4. What if 2 dragonflies fly away?
How many dragonflies would be left?

____ − ____ = ____

_____ dragonflies

Solve.

5. How many animals in all at the lake? _____ animals
1 more alligator comes.
How many animals are there now?

____ + ____ = ____

6. How many more swans than alligators do you see?

____ − ____ = ____

_____ more swan

Order Property and Zero Property

 How many in all?

1. $3 + 7 = $ _____

$7 + 3 = $ _____

2. $1 + 5 = $ _____

$5 + 1 = $ _____

 Write a number sentence to solve.

3. Use the picture. What 2 facts can you write?

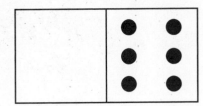

_____ + _____ = _____

_____ + _____ = _____

4. Use the picture. What 2 facts can you write?

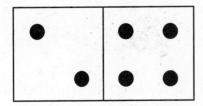

_____ + _____ = _____

_____ + _____ = _____

 Write a number sentence to solve.

5. Josh knows that $7 + 0 = 7$. How can Josh use the same addends and sum to write the fact another way?

_____ + _____ = _____

6. Emma knows that $4 + 5 = 9$. How can Emma use the same addends and sum to write the fact another way?

_____ + _____ = _____

Count On to Add

0 1 2 3 4 5 6 7 8 9 10

Solve.

1. How can you count on from 4?

   4 + 1 = _____

   4 + 2 = _____

   4 + 3 = _____

2. How can you count on from 6?

   6 + 1 = _____

   6 + 2 = _____

   6 + 3 = _____

Use the number line to solve.

3. Count on to add 5 + 2. What is the sum?

   5 + 2 = _____

4. Count on to add 3 + 7. What is the sum?

   3 + 7 = _____

Circle numbers on the number line above to solve.

5. Liu wants to add 2 + 8. How can she use the number line to solve?

   2 + 8 = _____

6. Dirk needs to add 7 + 1. How can he use the number line to solve?

   7 + 1 = _____

Addition Patterns

 **Use a pattern to solve.**

1. How can Mark add 3?
Complete.

1 + 3 = _____
2 + 3 = _____
3 + 3 = _____
4 + 3 = _____

2. How can Mia add 4?
Complete.

2 + 4 = _____
4 + 4 = _____
6 + 4 = _____
8 + 4 = _____

Complete the table to solve.

3. Mrs. Allen adds 3 to each number. Find the out number.

In	Out
1	
3	
5	
7	

4. Mr. Snow adds 5 points to each score. Find the out number.

In	Out
5	
6	
7	
8	

Use a table to solve.

5. Chris makes a table.
What rule does he use?

In	Out
5	5
10	10
15	15

The rule is _____

6. Kate makes a table.
What rule does she use?

In	Out
0	2
1	3
2	4

The rule is _____

© Macmillan/McGraw-Hill.

Write a number sentence to solve.

1. 5 black bears. 5 brown bears. 2 white bears. How many bears in all?

___ + ___ + ___ = ___

_____ bears

2. 2 cubs playing. 3 cubs sitting. 3 cubs sleeping. How many cubs in all?

___ + ___ + ___ = ___

_____ cubs

Add three numbers. Look for doubles or make 10.

3. Ellie feeds 3 lambs and 4 goats. Jack feeds 7 ducks. How many animals do they feed altogether?

_____ animals

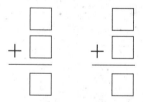

4. 6 penguins are on the low rocks and 4 are on the high rocks. 5 penguins are in the water. How many penguins are there in all?

_____ penguins

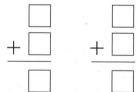

Write a number sentence to solve. Draw or write to explain.

5. Eric draws 1 giraffe, 6 pandas, and 6 lions. How many animals does he draw in all?

___ + ___ + ___ = ___

_____ animals

6. There are 9 boys, 3 teachers, and 7 girls watching the seals. How many people watch in all?

___ + ___ + ___ = ___

_____ people

© Macmillan/McGraw-Hill.

Draw a Picture

Draw a picture to solve.

1. 3 birds and 5 birds. How many birds in all?

_____ birds

2. 4 ducks and 3 ducks. How many ducks in all?

_____ ducks

Draw a picture to solve.

3. Julia sees 6 lions. Dave sees 1 more lion than Julia. How many lions do they see in all?

_____ lions

4. Nick counts 5 monkeys. Abby counts 2 fewer than Nick. How many monkeys do they count in all?

_____ monkeys

Draw a picture to solve. Use a shape for each animal.

5. In the bear house there are 5 brown bears and 3 black bears. There is 1 fewer grizzly bear than black bears. How many bears are there all together?

_____ bears

6. Nan counts 4 adult giraffes. Her sister counts 3 more young giraffes than adult giraffes. How many giraffes do they count in all?

_____ giraffes

Count Back to Subtract

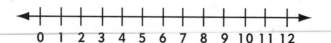

0 1 2 3 4 5 6 7 8 9 10 11 12

 **Count back to subtract. Use the number line to help.**

1. What is 4 − 2?

I start at _____. I count back _____ times. I land on _____. 4 − 2 = _____

2. What is 7 − 3?

I start at _____. I count back _____ times. I land on _____. 7 − 3 = _____

 Write a number sentence to solve. Use the number line.

3. There were 8 flowers in the garden. Tracey picked 3. How many flowers are left?

_____ − _____ = _____

_____ flowers are left.

4. 9 children were playing in the park. 2 went home. How many are left?

_____ − _____ = _____

_____ children are left.

 **Write a number sentence to solve. Use the number line.**

5. 12 boys and 3 girls went on a nature walk. How many more boys than girls went on the walk?

_____ − _____ = _____

_____ more boys

6. The vase has 11 roses, 3 daisies, and 2 tulips. How many more roses are there than daisies?

_____ − _____ = _____

_____ more roses

How many more roses than tulips?

_____ − _____ = _____

_____ more roses

Subtract All and Subtract Zero

 Circle the subtraction sentence that matches the story.

1. 5 birds are on a branch. None fly away. How many birds are on the branch?

$5 - 0 = 5$ $5 - 5 = 0$

2. 2 butterflies are on a flower. They both fly away. How many are left?

$2 - 2 = 0$ $2 - 0 = 2$

 Write a subtraction sentence to solve.

3. 12 children rode on the merry-go-round. They all got off. How many are on the merry-go-round now?

_____

_____ children

4. There were 8 ducks on the pond. None flew away. How many ducks are on the pond now?

_____

_____ ducks

 **Write a number sentence to solve.**

5. The squirrel had 7 nuts. Then it found 3 more. The squirrel did not eat any nuts. How many nuts does the squirrel have now?

_____

6. Write a story for this number sentence.

$5 - 5 = 0$

_____

Relate Addition to Subtraction

Circle the related subtraction fact. Then write the answer.

1.
$$5 + 1 = 6$$
$$5 - 1 = \underline{\quad} \quad 6 - 1 = \underline{\quad}$$

2.
$$7 + 3 = 10$$
$$10 - 3 = \underline{\quad} \quad 11 - 3 = \underline{\quad}$$

Write a number sentence. Then write a related fact.

3. 5 children played a game. 4 other children joined them. How many children are there now?

$$\underline{\quad} + \underline{\quad} = \underline{\quad}$$

$$\underline{\quad} - \underline{\quad} = \underline{\quad}$$

4. There were 4 birds in a nest. 2 flew away. How many birds are there now?

$$\underline{\quad} - \underline{\quad} = \underline{\quad}$$

$$\underline{\quad} + \underline{\quad} = \underline{\quad}$$

Solve.

5. Mike has 9 toy trucks. 2 trucks are blue. The rest are green. How many are green? Write the number sentence for the story.

$$\underline{\quad} - \underline{\quad} = \underline{\quad}$$

Then write a related addition fact.

$$\underline{\quad} + \underline{\quad} = \underline{\quad}$$

6. Write an addition story. Use the numbers 4, 6, and 10. Write the number sentence for your story.

$$\underline{\quad} + \underline{\quad} = \underline{\quad}$$

Then write a related subtraction fact.

$$\underline{\quad} - \underline{\quad} = \underline{\quad}$$

Missing Number

 Use related facts.

1. You have 6 apples. How many more apples do you need to have 8 apples?

$8 - 6 =$ ___ $6 + $ ___ $= 8$

You need _____ more apples.

2. Jay needs 9 pears. He has 5. How many more pears does he need?

$9 - 5 =$ ___ $5 + $ ___ $= 9$

Jay has to buy _____ more pears.

 Find the missing number. Write the related subtraction fact to solve.

3. 9 children play ball. 4 are girls. How many are boys?

$4 + $ ___ $= 9$ ___ $-$ ___ $=$ ___

_____ are boys.

4. There are 14 children at the party. 5 are boys. How many are girls?

$5 + $ ___ $= 14$ ___ $-$ ___ $=$ ___

_____ are girls.

 **Solve. Show your work.**

5. There are 15 balloons. They are red, white, and blue. 4 balloons are red. 6 balloons are white. How many are blue?

$4 + 6 =$ ___

$10 + $ ___ $= 15$ $15 - 10 =$ ___

_____ balloons are blue.

6. The girls have 20 jellybeans. Yoko has some. Pia has the same number. How many jellybeans does each girl have? Find the doubles.

___ $+$ ___ $= 20$

Names for Numbers

Circle the answers.

1. Which of these equal 8?

$6 - 2$ $2 + 6$ $8 + 0$

2. Which of these do not equal 3?

$2 - 1$ $5 - 2$ $3 + 3$

Solve.

3. There are 7 fish in the pond. Write number sentences that equal the number of fish.

_____ + _____ = _____

_____ − _____ = _____

_____ + _____ = _____

_____ − _____ = _____

4. There are 12 trees in the park. Write number sentences that equal the number of trees.

_____ + _____ = _____

_____ − _____ = _____

_____ + _____ + _____ = _____

_____ − _____ = _____

Solve.

5. 7 kites are flying. Write 3 addition facts to show the number of kites.

_____

_____

Write 3 subtraction facts to show the number of kites.

_____

_____

6. The children have cookies. Kim has 5 peanut butter. Mark has 4 chocolate. Perry has 2 oatmeal. How many cookies in all?

_____ + _____ + _____ = _____

Write 2 more addition facts to show the same number of cookies. _____

Write 2 subtraction facts to show the number of cookies.

_____

Problem Solving Skill:
Reading for Math

Read the story.
A Picnic

On the weekend, the park is full of people. The Nature Club will have a picnic in the park on Sunday. There are 6 boys in the club. There are 8 girls in the club.

 Solve.

1. When do you think the greatest number of people have picnics in the park?

Monday   Friday   Sunday

2. Which can you use to compare the number of girls in the club with the number of boys?

8 − 6   8 − 4   6 − 2

 Solve.

3. 9 children like cheese sandwiches. 5 children like peanut butter sandwiches. Write a subtraction sentence to compare the two groups.

____ − ____ = ____

____ more like cheese.

4. 10 children like orange juice. 4 children like apple juice. How many more children like orange juice than apple juice?

____ − ____ = ____

_____ more like orange.

 **Solve.**

5. 11 children go bird watching. 3 children go boating. How many more children go bird watching than boating?

____ − ____ = ____ more

6. 4 boys and 3 girls go on a hike. How many club members do <u>not</u> go on the hike?

_____ club members

Use Doubles to Add and Subtract

> **Use doubles to solve.**

1. Terri drew 8 snowflakes.
She drew 8 more.
What is the sum?

8 + 8 = _____

Terri drew one more.
What is the sum?

8 + 9 = _____

2. Derek has 5 rocks. Tom
gave him 5 more rocks.
What is the sum?

5 + 5 = _____

Derek gave the 5 rocks back.
What is the difference?

10 − 5 = _____

> **Solve.**

3. Tyler shows 9 with
counters. Tamika shows 9
too. What doubles fact do
they show?

_____ + _____ = _____

4. Sue wants to subtract
12 − 6.

What doubles fact can she
use to solve?

_____ + _____ = _____

12 − 6 = _____

> **Write a number sentence to solve.**

5. José had 14 letters to mail.
He mailed 7 letters. Write a
doubles fact can you use to
subtract 14 − 7.

_____ ◯ _____ ◯ _____

How many letters are left?

14 − 7 = _____ letters left

6. Marcy found 5 ladybugs on
a leaf. Lee found 1 more
ladybug than Marcy. How
many did they find?

_____ ◯ _____ ◯ _____

_____ ladybugs in all

Draw dots to solve.

1. Make 10 to help add
9 + 4.

10 + _____ = _____

9 + 4 = _____

2. Make 10 to help subtract
12 − 9.

12 − 10 = _____

12 − 9 = _____

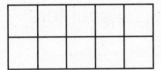

 Make 10 to help you solve.

3. Abby has 11 peanuts. She
eats 9 peanuts. How many
peanuts does she have left?

_____ − 10 = _____

11 − 9 = _____
Abby has _____
peanuts left.

4. David eats 9 grapes. Kyle
eats 5 grapes. How many
grapes do they eat in all?

10 + _____ = _____

9 + 5 = _____
They eat _____
grapes in all.

 Solve.

5. Paige has 9 cupcakes.
Melonie has 8 brownies.
How many sweets do they
have in all?

_____ ◯ _____ ◯ _____

_____ sweets in all

6. There are 13 pieces of
pizza. The children ate 9
pieces. How many pieces
of pizza are left?

_____ ◯ _____ ◯ _____

_____ pieces left

Use 10 to Add and Subtract 7 and 8

Draw dots to solve. Use a separate sheet of paper.

1. Peter needs to add $7 + 5$. First he shows 7 counters. How many counters does he put in the ten-frame to make 10?

   _____ counters

   $7 + 5 =$ _____

2. Noah wants to subtract $15 - 8$. He draws 10 dots on a ten-frame. He draws 5 dots under it. How many dots does he cross out?

   _____ dots

   $15 - 8 =$ _____

Make 10 to help you solve.

3. Mr. Tu bikes 8 miles on Saturday. He bikes 6 miles on Sunday. How many miles does he bike in all? Make 10 to help you solve.

   $10 +$ _____ $=$ _____

   $8 + 6 =$ _____
   He bikes _____ miles in all.

4. Mia buys 11 postcards. She sends 7 to friends. How many postcards does she have left? Make 10 to help you solve.

   _____ $- 10 =$ _____

   $11 - 7 =$ _____
   Mia has _____ postcards left.

Solve.

5. Adam walked 7 blocks to the park. Then he walked 4 blocks to the store. How many blocks did he walk to get to the store?

   _____ ◯ _____ ◯ _____

   _____ blocks

6. Shelly jumped rope 14 times. Casey jumped rope 8 times. How many more times did Shelly jump rope than Casey?

   _____ ◯ _____ ◯ _____

   _____ more times

Fact Families

 Complete the fact families.

1. 7 + 4 = _____

   11 − 7 = _____

   _____ + _____ = 11

   11 − _____ = 7

2. 6 + _____ = 13

   13 − _____ = 7

   _____ + _____ = 13

   _____ − _____ = 6

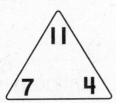

 Write the number sentences.

3. Lucas has 7 toy frogs and 8 toy snakes. He has 15 toys in all.
   Write the addition facts in this fact family.

   _____ + _____ = _____

   _____ + _____ = _____

4. Jonelle had 9 ribbons. Her Mom gave her 5 more. She has 14 in all.
   Write the subtraction facts in this fact family.

   _____ − _____ = _____

   _____ − _____ = _____

 Write number sentences to solve.

5. Lori made 7 bracelets. Then, she made 9 more. How many did Lori make in all?

   _____ + _____ = _____

   _____ bracelets in all

   Write three more number sentences in the fact family.

   _____ + _____ = _____

   _____ − _____ = _____

   _____ − _____ = _____

6. Frank has 17 marbles. Some are green. 8 are blue. How many are green?

   _____ − _____ = _____

   _____ green marbles

   Write three more number sentences in the fact family.

   _____ − _____ = _____

   _____ + _____ = _____

   _____ + _____ = _____

Problem Solving: Strategy
Write a Number Sentence

Write a number sentence to solve.

1. 18 geese are by the pond. 9 fly away. How many geese are left?

_____ ⊖ _____ ⊜ _____

_____ geese are left.

2. 9 boys and 8 girls are on a hike. How many children hike in all?

_____ ⊕ _____ ⊜ _____

_____ children in all

Write a number sentence to solve.

3. Tina finds 8 pinecones. Nan finds 7. How many pinecones do they find in all?

_____ ◯ _____ ◯ _____

_____ pinecones in all

4. The squirrels gather 12 acorns. They hide 4. How many acorns do they still have?

_____ ◯ _____ ◯ _____

_____ acorns

Write a number sentence to solve.

5. Two teachers share 14 orange slices for a snack. Ms. Jones eats 5 of the slices. How many of the slices does Mr. Hall eat?

_____ ◯ _____ ◯ _____

_____ slices

6. Joey finds 5 maple leaves and 2 oak leaves. Ali finds 6 elm leaves. How many leaves do they find in all?

_____ ◯ _____ ◯ _____ ◯ _____

_____ leaves in all

Use a picture to solve.

1. What number does Brian show?

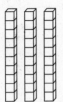

_____

2. What number does Kayla show?

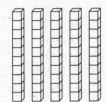

_____

 Draw a picture to solve. Use a separate sheet of paper.

3. Alex shows 2 groups of ten. What number does Alex show?

_____

4. Ken shows 7 groups of ten. What number does Ken show?

_____

 **Solve.**

5. Pilar had a roll of 50 pennies.

She put the pennies in groups of ten.

How many groups of ten does she have?

_____ groups of ten

6. Sean has 6 boxes of markers.

Each box has 10 markers.

How many markers does he have in all?

_____ markers

Use a picture to solve.

1. How many beans?

_____ beans

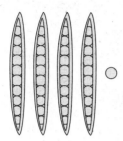

2. How many jacks?

_____ jacks

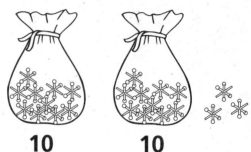

Write an addition sentence to solve.

3. Vicki uses cubes to show 7 tens and 5 ones.

What number does she show?

_____ + _____ = _____

4. Stefan uses cubes to show 9 tens and 3 ones.

What number does he show?

_____ + _____ = _____

 Draw a picture to solve. Use a separate sheet of paper.

5. Paige has 2 new boxes of markers.

There are 10 markers in each box.

She also has 5 markers in her desk.

How many markers in all does Paige have?

_____ markers

6. Mr. Hall has 4 packs of juice boxes.

Each pack has 10 juices.

How many juice boxes does Mr. Hall have in all?

_____ juice boxes

© Macmillan/McGraw-Hill.

Solve.

1. What is the value of the 6 in 61?

_____

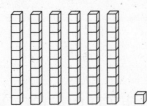

2. What is the value of the 2 in 52?

_____

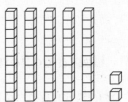

 Solve.

3. Rita shows the number 12 with place-value models.

She uses 2 ones.

How many tens does she use?

_____ ten

4. Drew shows the number 76 with place-value models.

He uses 7 tens.

How many ones does he use?

_____ ones

 Solve.

5. Zari asks, "What two numbers use the digits 3 and 1?"

What are the two numbers?

_____ and _____

Which of these numbers has 3 tens?

_____

6. Mr. Lo is thinking of a number.

The value of the ones digit is 8.

The value of the tens digit is 10.

What is Mr. Lo's number?

_____

Read and Write Numbers

Solve.

1. How can you write five as a number?

_____

2. How can you write fifty as a number?

_____

Use a pattern to solve.

3. Write each number word.

40 _____

41 _____

42 _____

43 _____

44 _____

45 _____

4. Write each number word.

95 _____

96 _____

97 _____

98 _____

99 _____

Draw a picture to solve. Use a separate sheet of paper.

5. The teacher asks you to show the number sixty-seven with place-value models.

How many tens will you use? _____ tens

How many ones? _____ ones

What number do you show? _____

6. Now show the number nineteen with place-value models.

How many tens will you use? _____ tens

How many ones? _____ ones

What number do you show? _____

Estimate Numbers

 Use estimation to solve.

1. About how many balls?

about _____ balls

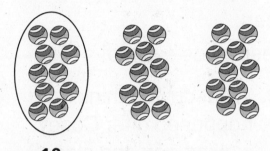

10

2. About how many jacks?

about _____ jacks

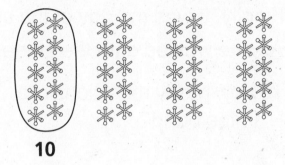

10

 Use estimation to solve.

3. Brian wants to eat about 20 peanuts. Circle the bag he should choose.

4. Leah needs about 50 chocolate chips to make muffins. Circle the bag she should choose.

Use estimation to solve.

5. About how many marbles will fill the bag?

about _____ marbles

10

6. About how many beans will fill the jar?

about _____ beans

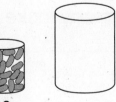

20

Problem Solving Skill: Reading for Math

> **Make predictions.**

Casey plays the trumpet in the band.

Each week the 20 musicians practiced.

Finally, it was the day of the concert.

As she walked onto the stage, Casey was excited!

1. How many musicians are in the band?

2. What do you think happened after Casey walked onto the stage?

_____ musicians

_____

> **Read the story above. Make predictions to solve.**

3. 11 of the musicians play the clarinet.

5 play the trumpet and the rest play the flute.

How many play the flute?

_____

4. The band practiced 15 pieces of music.

About how many pieces will they play in the concert?

about _____ pieces

> **Read the story above. Make predictions to solve.**

5. The musicians put their instruments in lockers.

Each locker can hold 2 instruments.

How many lockers did they use? _____ lockers

6. Casey's family paid $20.00 for 3 tickets to the concert.

Adult tickets cost $10.00. Children's tickets cost $5.00.

How many adult tickets did they buy? ____ ticket

How many children's tickets? _____ tickets

© Macmillan/McGraw-Hill.

Compare Numbers

> **Compare to solve.**

I. Anna's favorite number is 75.

Jack's is 60.

Which number is greater?

_____

2. Pete's favorite number is 99.

Lana's is 100.

Which number is less?

_____

> **Write greater than or less than. Then write < or >.**

3. Kyra has 53 flowers in her garden. Mara has 42 flowers.

53 is _____ 42.

53 ◯ 42

4. Rosa has 76¢. Taj has 85¢.

76¢ is _____ 85¢.

76¢ ◯ 85¢

> **Solve. Write <, >, or =.**

5. On Saturday, 92 people go to the zoo. On Sunday, 95 people go to the zoo.

92 ◯ 95

Were there more people on Saturday or on Sunday?

_____

6. Tariq has 9 blue cars and 8 red cars. Marty has 6 blue cars and 11 red cars. How many cars in all does Tariq have? _____ cars
How many cars in all does Marty have? _____ cars
Compare the number of cars the boys have.

____ ◯ ____

Order Numbers

 Write the number. Use a number line if you need help.

1. What number comes just before 100?

_____

2. Jon reads page 69 of his book.

He turns the page.

What page number is next?

_____

 Write the number. Use a number line if you need help.

3. Liz's age is between her brother's and her sister's.

Her brother is 9.

Her sister is 11.

How old is Liz?

_____

4. Mr. Morris gives clues about his age.

His age is more than 30.

It comes just before 40.

What is Mr. Morris's age?

_____

Draw a picture to solve. Use a separate sheet of paper.

5. Peng is making a map of his street. He wants to put the addresses in order from greatest to least.

The addresses are 33, 31, 32, 34.

How can he order the numbers? Draw 4 houses to help solve.

_____

6. Ms. Jones wants to put number cards in order from least to greatest.

The cards have the numbers 10, 5, 25, and 50.

How can she order the number cards? Draw the cards to help solve.

_____

Skip-Counting Patterns

Skip-count. Write the numbers.

1. Jim has a pile of dimes. What number could he use to skip-count and find how much money he has?

Skip-count by _____

2. How could Ms. Black skip-count to find how many eyes she sees in the classroom?

Skip-count by _____

Skip-count. Complete the pattern.

3. Tyler is making a game spinner. He starts at 10 and skip-counts by 5. Which numbers should he use to label the spinner parts?

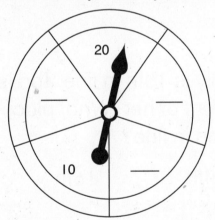

4. Mia is making a spinner for a game. She starts at 30 and skip-counts by 10. Which numbers should she use to label the spinner parts?

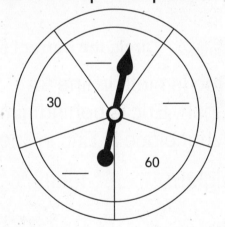

Skip-count to solve.

5. Ryan skip-counts by 5 four times. John skip-counts by 4 five times. They both start at 0 and stop at the same number. What is the number? _____

6. Megan skip-counts by 3 eight times. Sara skip-counts by 4 six times. They both start at 0 and stop at the same number. What is the number? _____

 **Use the map to solve. Write the answer.**

Leah made a map of the streets she crosses on the way to school.

50th	51st	52nd	53rd	54th	55th	56th

1. Which street does Leah cross after 50th?

_____

2. Which street comes before 55th street?

_____

 Circle the correct position.

3. Rob is ninth in line for lunch. Eric is behind him. What place is Eric in line?

eighth   tenth

4. Lily is 15th in line. Ian is in front of her. What place is Ian in line?

14th   16th

 Solve. Write the answer.

5. If today is the 20th of June, what date is tomorrow?

_____ of June

6. Monday was the first day of the month. What day was the fifth day?

_____

Even and Odd Numbers

 Find even and odd numbers to solve.

1. Write the missing even numbers.

38, _____, _____, 44

2. Write the missing odd numbers.

55, _____, 59, _____, 63

 Draw a picture to solve. Use a separate sheet of paper.

3. At school, 12 children stand in 2 lines for lunch. Can each child in line have a partner? _____

Is 12 an odd or even number? _____

4. At the soccer game, 25 children stand in 2 lines for tickets. Can each child have a partner? _____

Is 25 an odd or even number? _____

▭ **Use the picture to solve.**

5. Emma and Joey play a game with number cards. Emma picks 2 cards. She picks numbers that are odd and between 40 and 60. Circle the 2 cards she picks.

6. Joey picks 2 number cards. The numbers are even and between 70 and 90. Which cards does he pick? Mark with an X.

Problem Solving: Strategy
Use Logical Reasoning

Solve.

1. I am a number between 26 and 29. I am an odd number. What number am I?

   _____

2. I am a number greater than 90. I am an even number. I am less than 94. What number am I?

   _____

Use clues to solve.

3. Jade shows a color pattern with beads. White is next to red. Blue is next to white. Which color is in the middle?

   _____

4. Kim puts train cars in a row. The red car is behind the black car. The black car is behind the yellow car. Which color car is in front?

   _____

Draw or write to explain. Use a separate sheet of paper.

5. Four boys stand in line to buy sodas. Chad is third in line. Don is behind Chad. Allen is in front of Bob. Bob is second in line. Who is first in line?

   _____

6. Kyra has 3 doll houses. The white doll house is not the tallest. The purple doll house is the widest. The green doll house is the shortest. Which doll house is the tallest?

   _____

Pennies, Nickels, and Dimes

Draw coins to equal these amounts.

1. 5¢

15¢

2. 6¢

12¢

Solve. Draw to show your answer.

3. Mia buys an apple for 20¢. What coins can she use?

_____

4. Sam buys a plum for 17¢. What coins can he use?

_____

Solve a 2-step problem.

5. Judi shows 18¢ with nickels and pennies. How many nickels and pennies can she use?

___ nickels and ___ pennies

Tell how you can show 18¢ another way.

_____

6. Rao has 11¢ in dimes and pennies. How many dimes and pennies does he have?

___ dime and ___ penny

Tell how you can show 11¢ another way.

_____

Count Coin Collections

 Use a pattern to solve.

1. How much money?

_____¢

2. How much money?

_____¢

 **Use a model to solve.**

3. Tai has 3 dimes, 2 nickels, 3 pennies. Does he have enough money to buy the crab toy?

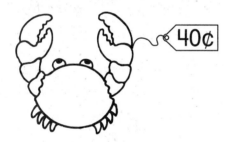

40¢

_____

4. Reese has 1 quarter, 4 dimes, 1 nickel. Does she have enough money to buy the starfish toy?

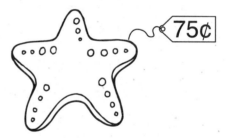

75¢

_____

 Solve a 2-step problem. Use a model if you need to.

5. Vance wants to buy a toy boat for 65¢. He has 2 quarters. His Dad gives him 1 dime and 1 nickel. Does he have enough money to buy the boat?

_____

6. Jose wants to buy a toy shark for 80¢. He has 1 half dollar. His Mom gives him 1 quarter. Does he have enough money to buy the shark?

_____

Money and Place Value

Use the table to solve.

Amount	Tens	Ones
5¢	0	5
10¢	1	0
15¢	1	5
20¢	2	0

1. How many tens do you use to show 20¢?

_____ tens

2. How many ones do you use to show 5¢?

_____ ones

Use coins to solve.

3. Ivan has 48¢. How can he show 48¢ as tens and ones?

_____ tens _____ ones

4. Eve has 55¢. How can she show 55¢ as tens and ones?

_____ tens _____ ones

Draw a picture to solve. Use a separate piece of paper.

5. Alana uses coins to show 3 tens and 1 one. Which coins does she use?

6. Kyle uses coins to show 1 ten and 3 ones. Which coins does he use?

Count each group of coins. Write the total amount.

1.

_____ ¢

_____ ¢

2.

_____ ¢

_____ ¢

Circle the correct group of coins to solve.

3. Which coins will pay for a 55¢ snack? Circle.

4. Which coins will pay for a 80¢ snack? Circle.

Solve.

5. Jill is at the toy store. She has 1 half dollar and 1 quarter. What is the most Jill can pay for a toy?

_____

6. Pete wants to buy a ticket at the fair. He has 2 quarters, 1 dime, and 2 nickels. What is the most he can pay for a ticket?

_____

Make Equal Amounts

 Draw a picture to solve. Use a separate sheet of paper.

1. How can you show 20¢ another way?

2. How can you show 12¢ another way?

 Draw a picture to solve.

3. Show two ways to make 26¢. Circle the way that uses fewer coins.

4. Show two ways to make 33¢. Circle the way that uses fewer coins.

Complete the table. Show how many of each coin you need.

5. Show 42¢ two more ways.

Quarter	Dime	Nickel	Penny
1	1	1	2

6. Show 61¢ two more ways.

Quarter	Dime	Nickel	Penny
			61

© Macmillan/McGraw-Hill.

Problem Solving Skill:
Reading for Math

yogurt...............75¢	
fruit..................24¢	
popcorn.............98¢	
bottled water.....82¢	
juice..................70¢	

Tony and his Mom spent two hours at the fair. "I'm hungry. Can we have a snack?" asked Tony. They stopped at the food stand and read the menu.

 Solve.

1. How many hours were Tony and his Mom at the fair?

_____

2. How much money does the yogurt cost?

_____¢

 Solve.

3. Which item on the menu costs the same as 3 quarters, 1 nickel, and 2 pennies?

_____

4. Why did they stop to read the menu?

_____

 **Solve.**

5. Tony chooses yogurt and fruit. How much money does he spend in all?

_____

6. Which item on the menu costs the least?

_____

Which item on the menu costs the most?

_____

© Macmillan/McGraw-Hill.

Use a picture to solve.

1. How much money does Tyler have?

_____ ¢

2. How much money does Sela have?

_____ ¢

Solve. Draw or write your answer.

3. How many quarters do you need to show one dollar?

_____ quarters

4. How many dimes do you need to show one dollar?

_____ dimes

Solve.

5. Rachel uses 20 of the same coin to show $1.00. Which coin does she use?

_____

6. Jim uses 100 of the same coin to show $1.00. Which coin does he use?

_____

Use a picture to solve.

1. How much money does Tim have?

$____ . ____

2. How much money does Ellie have?

$____ . ____

 Solve. Draw a picture if you need help. Use a separate sheet of paper.

3. Mary has 1 dollar, 1 dime, and 4 pennies to buy a snack. How much money does she have?

$____ . ____

4. Ben has 2 dollars, 1 quarter, and 2 dimes to buy lunch. How much money does he have?

$____ . ____

Solve a 2-step problem.

5. Ali buys a toy for $1.75. He pays with dollars and quarters. How many of each did he use?

____ dollars and ____ quarters

What is another way Ali could pay $1.75?

_____

6. Greg buys a toy for $2.20. He pays with dollars and dimes. How many of each did he use?

____ dollars and ____ dimes

What is another way he could pay $2.20?

_____

Compare Money Amounts

 Use a picture to solve.

1. Is this enough money to buy a $1.00 toy?

_____

2. Is this enough money to buy a $1.50 toy?

_____

 Use a picture to solve.

3. Count the money Nora has in her purse. Is it enough to buy a toy panda for $2.00?

_____

4. Count Derek's money. Is it enough to buy a toy dinosaur for $1.49?

_____

 Solve a 2-step problem. Use a model to solve.

5. Marta wants to buy a book that costs $1.79. She has 1 dollar, 3 quarters, and 1 dime. How much money does Marta have? $____.____

Does she have enough money to buy the book?

_____

6. Riley wants to buy a kite for $1.25. He has 1 dollar, 1 dime, and 10 pennies. How much money does Riley have? $____.____

Does he have enough money to buy the kite?

_____

Make Change

> **Solve.**

1. You pay 25¢ for a 23¢ toy.
Do you get change?

_____

2. You pay 40¢ for a 40¢ toy.
Do you get change?

_____

> **Solve. Use coins if you need help.**

3. Sophie buys seeds for 19¢.
She gives Mr. Smith 2
dimes. How much change
does she get back?

_____¢

4. Cody buys a pot for 47¢.
He gives Mr. Smith 2
quarters. How much
change does he get back?

_____¢

> **Draw a picture to solve. Use a separate sheet of paper.**

5. Sonia and Tess play store.
Sonia gives Tess 3 dimes
for a 28¢ toy. What coins
should Tess give Sonia as
change?

_____

6. Jade sells a cup of
lemonade for 20¢ to a friend.
He gives Jade 1 quarter.
What coins should Jade
give as change?

_____

Problem Solving: Strategy
Act it Out

Act it out to solve.

1. You have 1 dime. You buy a sticker for 5¢. How much change should you get?

_____ ¢ change

2. Dad has 1 quarter. He buys a 20¢ paper. How much change should he get?

_____ ¢ change

Act it out to solve.

3. Jared has 4 quarters. He buys cards for 89¢. How much change should he get?

_____ ¢ change

4. Clara has a 1 dollar bill. She buys a pencil for 75¢. How much change should she get?

_____ ¢ change

Solve.

5. Jim has 1 half dollar. His Mom gives him 1 quarter. He buys a marker for 70¢. How much change should he get?

_____ ¢ change

6. Anna has 2 quarters and Jesse has 5 dimes. They combine their money to buy drawing paper for 99¢. How much change should they get back?

_____ ¢ change

Time to the Hour and Half Hour

Draw the hands to show each time.

1. Show 6:00.

2. Show 10:30.

 Draw the hands to show each time.

3. Where are the hands on the clock when Nick goes to school at 9:00?

4. Where are the hands on the clock when Rosa eats dinner at 5:30?

 **Use estimation.**

5. Ian wakes up at 7:00. It takes him about 1 hour to get ready for school. At about what time is Ian ready?

about _____ : _____

6. Ali starts reading at eight-thirty. She reads for a half hour before going to sleep. At about what time does Ali go to sleep?

about _____ : _____

Time to Five Minutes

1. What time does the clock show? _____:_____

2. What time does the clock show? _____:_____

Skip-count by 5s to solve.

3. Vic counts by 5 to help him tell time.

10: 00, 10:05, 10:10

What time comes next?

_____:_____

4. Lisa counts by 5 to help her tell time.

11:30, 11: 35, 11: 40.

What time comes next?

_____:_____

Draw a picture to solve. Use a separate sheet of paper. Tell how you got your answer.

5. Don looks at the clock. The hour hand is on 8. The minute hand is on 1. What time does Don see on the clock? _____:_____

_____

_____

6. Diana looks at the clock. The hour hand is on 4. The minute hand is on 5. What time does Diana see on the clock? _____:_____

_____

_____

Time to the Quarter Hour

Draw a picture to solve. Use a separate sheet of paper.

1. What number does the minute hand point to at 6:15? _____

2. What number does the minute hand point to at 7:45? _____

Use a pattern to solve.

3. The bell rings every 15 minutes during swim practice.

10:00, 10:15, 10:30.

At what time will the bell ring next?

_____ : _____

4. The bird comes out of the clock every 15 minutes. Hannah sees it at 3:30 and 3:45.

At what time will the bird come out next?

_____ : _____

Solve.

5. Brett needs to be at soccer practice at 4:15. It takes about 15 minutes to walk to the field. At what time should he leave for practice?

_____ : _____

6. Jenna is going to a party that begins at 1:00. It will take her Mom 15 minutes to drive her to the party. At what time should they leave for the party?

_____ : _____

Time Before and After the Hour

Solve. Write each time two ways.

1. What is the time?

| 8:15 |

_____ minutes after _____

a quarter after _____

2. What is the time?

| 2:45 |

_____ minutes after _____

_____ minutes before _____

Write each time more than one way. Draw a picture to help. Use a separate sheet of paper.

3. Sally says that the clock shows 50 minutes after 11. What is another way to write the time?

_____

4. Paul tells the time as 30 minutes before 9. What is another way to write the time?

_____

Circle the unneccessary information. Then draw or write to solve. Explain your answer.

5. Mark goes to bed at 8:30. Kevin stays up to a quarter after 8. The brothers have a snack at 8:00. Who goes to bed first? _____

6. The clock shows 5:45. Dance lessons begin at 6:00. Olivia reads the time as 15 minutes before 6. Julia reads it as 15 minutes after 5. Who is right?

_____

Problem Solving Skill: Reading for Math

At 10:15 in the morning, my family got on the train to the city. The train ride took 45 minutes. When we arrived at the city, we ate lunch. At 2:00 it was time for the music show. The show ended at 4: 30. Then we took the train home.

1. What time did the family get on the train?

_____

2. When did the show end?

_____

3. What time did the train arrive in the city?

_____

4. What was the last thing the family did?

_____

5. How long was the music show?

_____

6. What did the family do first when they arrived in the city?

_____

A.M. and P.M.

 Write A.M. or P.M.

1. Nan eats breakfast. What time of the day is it?

It is 8:00 _____.

2. Rick gets ready for bed. What time is it?

It is 9:00 _____.

 Write A.M. or P.M.

3. Diaz is taking a walk. The sun is setting. It is getting dark. What time is it?

It is 6:00 _____.

4. Mia is on her way to the park. She is going to meet her friends. They are going to have a picnic. What time is it?

It is 12:30 _____.

Answer each question. Remember to write A.M. or P.M.

5. Bob has to wake up at 7:00 A.M. Two hours later school will start. What time will school start? School will start at _____. What number sentence can you write to figure out the time?

_____

6. Lanie is watching a movie. The movie started at 11:00 A.M. It is three hours long. When will the movie end? Use the clock to help.

The movie will end at _____.

Elapsed Time

Answer each question. Use the 🕐 to help you.

1. The dance lesson starts at 10:00 A.M. It ends at 11:00 A.M. How long does the lesson last? _____ hour

2. The game started at 2:00 P.M. It ended at 4:00 P.M. How much time passed? _____ hours have passed.

Answer each question. Use the 🕐 to help you.

3. Mei and Troy build a fort. They started at 1:00 P.M. They finished at 4:00 P.M. How many hours have passed?

_____ hours have passed

4. Joey goes for a horse ride. He leaves at 8:00 A.M. and gets back at noon. How long does the horse ride last?

_____ hours

Solve.

5. Draw the hands on the clock to show each time.

Rosa is going on a trip to the lake. The bus leaves at 9:00 A.M. It gets to the lake at 1:00 P.M. How long does it take to get to the lake?

_____ hours

6. Joni leaves Sara's house at 1:00 P.M. and goes to Lucy's house. She leaves Lucy's house at 2:00 P.M. and goes to Trish's house. Joni gets home at 4:00 P.M. How many hours passed since Joni left Sara's house?

_____ hours have passed.

Calendar

 Use the calendar to answer each question.

December	January	February
S M T W T F S	S M T W T F S	S M T W T F S
1 2 3 4 5 6	1 2 3	1 2 3 4 5 6 7
7 8 9 10 11 12 13	4 5 6 7 8 9 10	8 9 10 11 12 13 14
14 15 16 17 18 19 20	11 12 13 14 15 16 17	15 16 17 18 19 20 21
21 22 23 24 25 26 27	18 19 20 21 22 23 24	22 23 24 25 26 27 28
28 29 30 31	25 26 27 28 29 30 31	

1. Which month starts on a Monday?

2. Paul's birthday is in the month with 28 days. In which month is his birthday?

_____

_____

 Use the calendar to answer each question.

3. Which month has the most Tuesdays?

4. Jeff will go to the dentist on January 21st. On which day of the week will he go?

_____

_____

 **Use the calendar to answer each question.**

5. Susan is going to her aunt's house on the first Monday in January. What is the date?

6. Alice is going to her grandmother's house on February 7th. She is staying for two weeks. On which day will she go home?

_____

_____

Time Relationships

Write minutes or hours.

1. Casey wants to make a sandwich. How long will it take her?

3 _____

2. Andy hikes through the woods. How long is his hike?

I _____

Write days or months.

3. Ms. Down is on vacation. She is taking a short trip. How long will she be gone?

10 _____

4. It is Linda's birthday today. How long will she have to wait before her next birthday?

12 _____

Circle the answer to each question.

5. Jennifer has a baby brother. He is I year old. He is about 12 _____ old.

days   weeks   months

6. Marty wanted to build a tree house. His older brother helped him. It took them I month to finish it. It took them about 30 _____ to finish it.

hours   days   weeks

Problem Solving: Strategy
Use a Model

 Use the calendar to solve.

1. Ben got a puppy on the first Saturday in April. What is the date?

April _____

2. The bicycle race is on the third Sunday in January. What is the date?

January _____

December							January							February					
S	M	T	W	T	F	S	S	M	T	W	T	F	S	S	M	T	W	T	F	S

December
S M T W T F S
1 2 3 4 5 6
7 8 9 10 11 12 13
14 15 16 17 18 19 20
21 22 23 24 25 26 27
28 29 30 31

January
S M T W T F S
1
2 3 4 5 6 7 8
9 10 11 12 13 14 15
16 17 18 19 20 21 22
23 24 25 26 27 28 29
30 31

February
S M T W T F S
1 2 3 4 5
6 7 8 9 10 11 12
13 14 15 16 17 18 19
20 21 22 23 24 25 26
27 28

March
S M T W T F S
1 2 3 4 5
6 7 8 9 10 11 12
13 14 15 16 17 18 19
20 21 22 23 24 25 26
27 28 29 30 31

April
S M T W T F S
1 2
3 4 5 6 7 8 9
10 11 12 13 14 15 16
17 18 19 20 21 22 23
24 25 26 27 28 29 30

May
S M T W T F S
1 2 3 4 5 6 7
8 9 10 11 12 13 14
15 16 17 18 19 20 21
22 23 24 25 26 27 28
29 30 31

 **Use the calendar above to solve.**

3. The class will have a talent show on the second Tuesday in May. What is the date?

Tuesday, May _____

4. Adam's party is on the last day in March. Write the day of the week and the date of the party.

_____

Use the calendar above to solve.

5. On Sunday, April 10th, Jay starts swimming lessons. Two weeks later, he starts drumming lessons. On which day of the week and date does he start his drumming lessons?

_____

6. Grace was born on February 25th. Her best friend Anne was born 10 days later. When is Anne's birthday?

_____

© Macmillan/McGraw-Hill

Picture and Bar Graphs

 Use the picture graph to solve.

The graph shows votes for our favorite ball game.

Favorite Ball Game	
Baseball	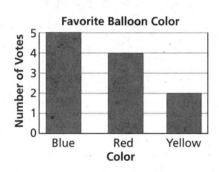
Basketball	
Football	

Key: Each ball is 1 vote.

1. How many people voted?

_____ people

2. How many more liked baseball than football?

_____ people

 Use the bar graph to solve.

The bar graph shows our votes for favorite balloon color.

Favorite Balloon Color

3. What is the favorite color?

_____

4. How many more votes did red get than yellow?

_____ more votes

Use the bar graph to solve.

Raul's class voted on their favorite art activity. There are 22 children in the class.

5. The graph is not yet finished. How many more votes should the graph show? _____ more votes

The rest of the class voted for sculpting. Color the graph to show how many voted for sculpting.

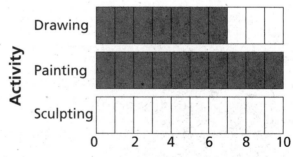

Favorite Art Activity

6. How many more children voted for painting than sculpting?

_____ more children

© Macmillan/McGraw-Hill

Surveys

Solve.

1. You want to take a survey about favorite games. Which question should you ask? Put a ✓ beside your answer.
   ___ Where do you like to play?
   ___ What is your favorite game?
   ___ Who are your friends?

2. You finished your survey about favorite games. You asked 7 children. How many tally marks will your chart show?

   _____ tally marks

Use the chart to solve.

3. Adam asked friends to vote on their favorite game. Write the total number of votes for each game.

Game	Tally	Total
Tag	II	
Catch	IIII	
Hide-and-seek	II	

4. Which game received the most votes?

   _____

Complete the chart to solve.

Favorite Amusement Ride	Tally	Total
Roller Coaster	IIIII	6
Ferris Wheel	IIIIIIII	10
Bumper Cars	IIII	4

5. Which ride got the most votes? _____
   Which ride got the least votes? _____

6. How many more people voted for the Ferris wheel than the bumper cars?
   _____ more people

Make a Bar Graph

Use the bar graph to solve.

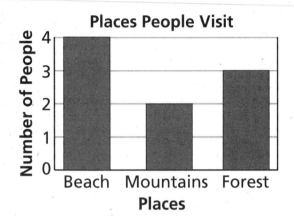

Places People Visit

1. How many people visited the beach?

   _____ people

2. How many people visited the forest?

   _____ people

Use the bar graph to solve each problem.

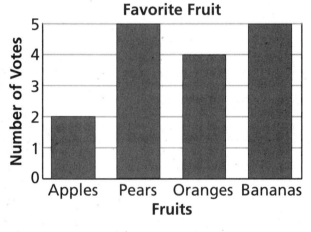

Favorite Fruit

3. Which fruit or fruits got the most votes?

   _____

4. Which got the fewest votes?

   _____

   How many votes did this fruit get?

   _____ votes

Use the graph above to solve each problem.

5. How many more votes did oranges get than apples? Write a number sentence to compare.

   _____ − _____ = _____

   _____ more votes

6. How many people voted in all? Write the number sentence to find out.

   ___ + ___ + ___ + ___ = ___

   _____ people voted in all.

Pictographs

Use the pictograph to solve the problems.

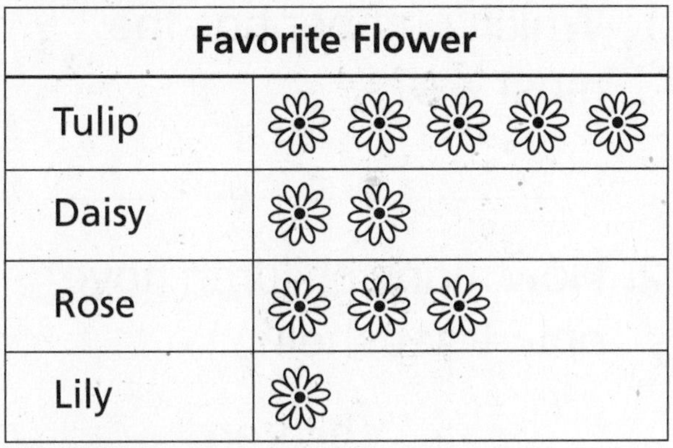

Favorite Flower	
Tulip	❀ ❀ ❀ ❀ ❀
Daisy	❀ ❀
Rose	❀ ❀ ❀
Lily	❀

Each ❀ stands for 2 votes

1. Which flower got the most votes?

_____

2. How many votes did the lily get?

_____ votes

3. Which flower got 6 votes?

_____

4. How many total votes did the daisy and the rose get?

_____ votes

5. How many more votes did the tulip get than the daisy? Write a number sentence to find out.

_____

The tulip got _____ more votes than the daisy.

6. What if each ❀ stands for I vote? How many votes in all would be in the graph?

_____ votes

Use the line plot to solve each problem.

Number of Seashells We Have

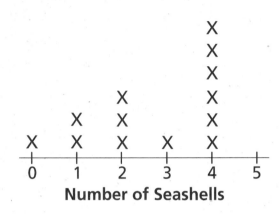

1. Which number has the most X's?

_____

2. How many children have only 1 seashell?

_____ children

Use the Seashells line plot above to solve.

3. Finish the line plot. Show that 5 people have 5 seashells.

4. Now how many children have more than 3 seashells?

_____ children

Make a line plot and solve. Use a separate sheet of paper.

Draw a line plot. Title it, "Number of Comic Books We Have." Show that 3 children have 1 comic book, and 2 have 2 comic books. Show that no children have 3 comic books, and that 5 children have 4 comic books. Show that one child has 5 comic books.

5. How many children have fewer than 3 comic books?

_____ children

6. How many children have more than 3 comic books?

_____ children

© Macmillan/McGraw-Hill

Different Ways to Show Data

 Use the pictograph to solve.

Favorite Snacks	
Candy	● ● ●
Popcorn	●
Cookies	● ●

Each ● stands for 2 votes

1. How many children voted for popcorn?

_____ children

2. How many votes did candy get?

_____ votes

 Complete the tally chart and solve.

3. Use the information above to finish the tally chart.

4. How many more children voted for candy than popcorn? Write a number sentence.

_____ – _____ = _____

_____ children

Favorite Snacks		
Snack	Tally	Total
Candy		
Popcorn		
Cookies		

Complete the bar graph and solve.

5. Use the information from the pictograph and tally chart. Finish the bar graph.

6. Which snack got the greatest number of votes?

_____

Which graph did you use to answer? Explain.

_____

Problem Solving Skill:
Reading for Math

 **Use the tally chart to solve.**

Favorite Vegetable		
Vegetable	Tally Marks	Total
Corn	ⲧⲏⲧ	5
Green beans	llll	4
Spinach	ⲧⲏⲧll	7

1. Which vegetable had the most votes? _____

2. Did more children vote for green beans or corn?

_____

How many more? _____

Solve.

3. 5 girls voted for math. 2 boys voted for math. How many more girls voted for math?

_____ girls

4. 7 children voted for art. 5 children voted for reading. How many more children voted for art?

_____ children

Use the tally chart to solve.

Favorite Sport		
Sport	Tally Marks	Total
Running	ⲧⲏⲧ ⲧⲏⲧ	10
Biking	llll	4
Skating	ⲧⲏⲧ	5

5. How many children voted in all?

_____ children

6. How many more children voted for running than biking?

_____ children

Use a picture to solve.

1. Jean trades ones to make a ten. How many tens and ones will she show?

_____ ten _____ ones

2. Sid can trade ones. How many tens and ones will he show?

_____ tens _____ ones

Solve.

3. Kate has 20 ones. She trades them for tens. How many tens will she get?

_____ tens

4. Rob shows 1 ten and 15 ones. He regroups ones. How many tens and ones does he show now?

_____ tens _____ ones

Solve.

5. Jon has 32 ones. He regroups ones for tens. How many tens will he get?

_____ tens

6. Bethany had 10 stickers. Tara had 9 stickers. Write 2 ways you can show all the stickers with tens and ones.

_____

Addition with Sums to 20

Solve. Use ▭ and ▭▭▭▭▭▭ if you need help.

1. Alexi needs to add 6 + 8. Show 6 ones and 8 ones. Can he regroup ones to make a ten? _____

What is the sum?

6 + 8 = _____

2. Ally needs to add 9 + 6. She shows 9 ones and 6 ones. Can she regroup ones to make a ten? _____

What is the sum?

9 + 6 = _____

Solve. Use ▭ and ▭▭▭▭▭▭ if you need help.

3. Jen had 9 markers. She bought 9 more. How many markers does Jen have now?

9 + 9 = _____ markers

4. Ara found 7 ladybugs on a leaf. She found 8 butterflies on a tree. How many insects did she find in all?

7 + 8 = _____ insects

Solve. Use ▭ and ▭▭▭▭▭▭ if you need help.

5. Lu drew 7 spaceships. Michael drew 2 more spaceships than Lu. How many spaceships did Michael draw? _____ spaceships

How many spaceships in all did Lu and Michael draw?

7 + __ = __ spaceships in all

6. There are 11 red marbles in a box. There are 3 fewer blue marbles than red marbles.

How many blue marbles are there? _____ marbles

How many red and blue marbles are in the box?

11 + __ = __ red and blue marbles

Addition with Greater Numbers

 Use a picture to solve. Use 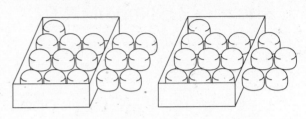 and if you need help.

1. How many markers in all?

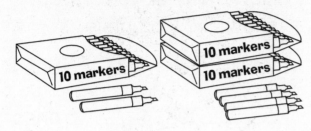

_____ markers

2. How many rolls in all?

_____ rolls

Solve. Use and if you need help.

3. There are 17 party hats. There are 24 whistles. Can you regroup ones? _____

How many hats and whistles in all?

17 + 24 = ____ hats and whistles

4. There were 33 poodles at the dog show. There were 26 bull dogs. Can you regroup the ones? _____

How many poodles and bull dogs in all? 33 + 26 = ____ poodles and bull dogs

Solve.

5. Rachel makes 27 milk chocolates and 15 dark chocolates. How many chocolates does she have in all? _____

She puts them into boxes of 10. How many boxes of 10 can she fill? _____ boxes

How many chocolates does she have left over? _____

6. Justin has 16 football cards and 24 baseball cards. How many cards does he have in all? _____

Each sheet in his notebook holds 10 cards.

How many sheets of 10 can he fill? _____ sheets

How many cards does he have left over? _____

Renaming Numbers

Write different ways to show each number.

1. How many ways can you show 19? Complete.

   _____ ten _____ ones

   _____ ten _____ ones

2. How many ways can you show 25? Complete.

   _____ ten _____ ones

   _____ ten _____ ones

   _____ ten _____ ones

Solve.

3. Ray shows a number with 1 ten and 18 ones. Write other ways to show Ray's number.

   _____ tens _____ ones

   _____ tens _____ ones

   _____

4. Chen shows the number 23 in different ways. What are some ways Chen might show 23?

   _____ tens _____ ones

   _____ ten _____ ones

   _____

Use a pattern to solve.

5. Rosa shows 1 ten 17 ones. Olivia shows 37 ones. Dora shows 2 tens 7 ones. Which girls show the same number?

   _____

6. Alana shows the number 34 with ones. What are some other ways she can show 34? Show them.

   _____

Problem Solving: Strategy
Use a Pattern

 Use a pattern to solve.

1. The baker baked 5 cakes. He bakes 25 more. How many cakes in all?

$5 + 5 = 10$

$5 + 15 =$ ____

$5 + 25 =$ ____ cakes

2. The baker sold 7 pies on Friday. He sold 34 pies on Saturday. How many pies did he sell in all?

$7 + 14 = 21$

$7 + 24 =$ ____

$7 + 34 =$ ____ pies

 Use a pattern to solve.

3. Ms. Shaw buys fruit bars. She buys 5 berry and 36 lemon bars. How many fruit bars does she buy all together?

$5 + 6 = 11$

___ + ___ = ___

___ + ___ = ___

___ + ___ = ___ fruit bars

4. There are only 6 brownies on the tray. The baker makes 24 more. How many brownies are there now?

$6 + 4 = 10$

___ + ___ = ___

___ + ___ = ___ brownies

 Use a pattern to solve.

5. Zoe's family drove 8 miles to the store. Then they drove 25 more miles to the park. How many miles in all did they drive?

___ + ___ = ___ miles

6. Mr. Neff goes to the bagel store. He buys 9 big bagels and 24 mini-bagels. How many bagels does he buy all together?   ____ bagels

Add Tens

> **Write a number sentence to solve.**

1. Erica has 10 apples. Dan has 10 apples.

How many apples do they have together?

_____ apples

_____ + _____ = _____

2. Stella has 20 cents. Her dad gives her 10 cents.

How many cents does she have in all?

_____ cents

_____ + _____ = _____

> **Use the number line to solve.**

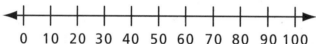

3. Yat has 30 blue marbles and 20 red marbles. How many marbles does he have in all? Start at _____.
Add _____. Where do you land? _____
Yat has _____ marbles.

4. The baker baked 50 blueberry muffins and 20 chocolate chip muffins. How many muffins did he bake in all? Start at _____.
Add _____. Where do you land? _____
He baked _____ muffins.

> **Solve. Use the number line above if you need help.**

5. Evan had 50 stickers. Then added 10. Then added 20 more. How many did he have in all?

50 + 10 + 20 = _____

6. Gila has 3 dimes. She found 2 dimes in her coat pocket. She wants to change all her dimes for pennies. How many pennies will she get?

_____ pennies

Count on Tens and Ones to Add

 Use the number line. Count on to add.

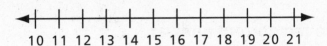
10 11 12 13 14 15 16 17 18 19 20 21

1. Grace has 16 red buttons. She has 3 blue buttons. How many buttons does she have in all? Start at 16. Count on _____.
Where do you land? _____
Grace has _____ buttons.

2. Armand drew 19 pictures. Then he drew 2 more. How many pictures did he draw in all? Start at _____. Count on _____.
Where do you land? _____
Armand has _____ pictures.

 Use the hundred chart. Then circle the correct answer.

1	2	3	4	5	6	7	8	9	10
11	12	13	14	15	16	17	18	19	20
21	22	23	24	25	26	27	28	29	30
31	32	33	34	35	36	37	38	39	40
41	42	43	44	45	46	47	48	49	50
51	52	53	54	55	56	57	58	59	60
61	62	63	64	65	66	67	68	69	70
71	72	73	74	75	76	77	78	79	80
81	82	83	84	85	86	87	88	89	90
91	92	93	94	95	96	97	98	99	100

3. Darin had 17 baseball cards. His sister gave him 2 more cards. How many cards does he have now?

15   19   21

4. Heidi is having a party. She wrote 24 invitations on Tuesday. She wrote 10 more on Wednesday. How many did she write in all?

25   34   35

 Use the hundred chart to solve.

5. How much is $45 + 10 + 10$?
_____ Did you move **across** or **down** the chart to add tens? _____

6. How much is $47 + 3 + 20$?
_____ Did you move **across** or **down** the chart to add $47 + 3$? _____
How did you move to add 20 to that? _____

Decide When to Regroup

1. There are 12 red blocks and 6 white blocks. How many are there in all?

   8   16   18

2. Ida has 15 shells. Rod has 8 shells. How many do they have together?

   13   23   28

Solve.

3. Sue has 32 blue marbles and 7 yellow marbles. How many marbles does she have in all?

   _____ marbles

   Did you regroup to add?
   Yes   No

4. Ben collects rocks. He has 46 rocks. Today he found 7 more rocks. How many rocks does he have in all?

   _____ rocks

   Did you regroup to add?
   Yes   No

Solve.

5. If you add 75 and 6, will the sum be less than or greater than 80?

   _____

   What is the sum of 75 and 6?

   _____

6. There were 22 cups on the shelf. Trish added 3 more. Hank added 3 more. How many cups are on the shelf?

   _____ cups

   Did you need to regroup? Explain.

   _____

Add a 1-Digit and a 2-Digit Number

> **Write a number sentence to solve.**

1. Rita counts 12 cans in one box, and 7 cans in another box. How many cans does she count in all?

_____ + _____ = _____ cans

Did you regroup? Write Yes or No.

_____

2. Jimmy washed 16 blue socks and 6 red socks. How many socks did he wash in all?

_____ + _____ = _____ socks

Did you regroup? Write Yes or No.

_____

> **Solve. Show your work. Use a separate sheet of paper.**

3. There were 24 ducks on a pond. Then 7 more ducks joined them. How many ducks were there in all?

_____ ducks

4. The baker has 35 corn and 8 bran muffins.
How many muffins does she have in all?

_____ muffins

> **Solve. Use a separate sheet of paper to show your work.**

5. Dee has 56 picture books. For her birthday, she got 9 more books. Her bookshelf can hold 65 books. Will all her books fit on her shelf? How do you know?

_____

_____

6. Ms. Benson bought a big cake and a small cake for her party. The big cake serves 15. The small cake serves 8. She invited 27 people. Should she buy another small cake? Why?

_____

_____

Add 2-Digit Numbers

Solve.

1. 10 boys and 13 girls went to the museum. How many children went to the museum in all?

_____ children

2. Derek counts 23 red chairs and 18 blue chairs. How many chairs in all does Derek count?

_____ chairs

Solve.

3. This morning, Nina spent 25 minutes on the computer. This afternoon, she spent 37 minutes. How many minutes did she spend on the computer in all?

_____ minutes

4. Alfred's dad drove 53 miles from Mapleton to Sienna. Then he drove 11 miles to Palmer. How many miles did he drive from Mapleton to Palmer?

_____ miles

Solve.

5. Toni picked 54 berries. Lulu picked 43 berries. How many berries in all did they pick? Write a number sentence.

___ + ___ = ___ berries

They need 40 berries to bake pies. Can they bake 2 pies? Explain.

6. Sandy wants to buy a pen. It costs 87 cents. She has 6 dimes, 1 nickel, and 22 pennies. Does she have enough money to buy the pen? Explain.

_____

_____

_____

_____

Practice Addition

Sunny Valley School is having a Fun Fair.

Read and solve. Use a separate sheet of paper.

1. 18 boys and 15 girls painted the banner for the fair. How many children painted the banner?

   _____ children

2. There are 14 chocolate cupcakes and 13 lemon cupcakes. How many cupcakes in all?

   _____ cupcakes

Solve.

3. In the morning, 32 cups of lemonade were sold. In the afternoon, 28 cups were sold. How many cups were sold in all?

   _____ cups

4. The art show at the fair had 23 pictures in one room. There were 52 pictures in another room. How many pictures were there in all?

   _____ pictures

Solve.

5. Ben spends 30 cents on lemonade and 55 cents on a snack. Tia also buys lemonade and a snack that costs 65 cents. How much does each one spend?

   Ben spends _____ cents.

   Tia spends _____ cents.

6. On Tuesday, the fair took in 43 dollars. On Wednesday, the fair took in 50 dollars. How many dollars did the fair take in on Tuesday and Wednesday all together?

   _____ dollars

   Explain how to count on by tens to find out. _____

   _____

Problem Solving: Reading for Math

The Flower Club had $45. They sold some flowers and got $16 more. The students made a list of supplies to buy for the club.

Read about the Flower Club and answer each question.

1. What does the Flower Club make a list of?

_____

2. How much money does the club have to spend in all?

_____ dollars

Read about the Flower Club and solve.

3. The Flower Club buys a shovel that costs $16. They buy a pail that costs $7. How much do the shovel and pail together cost?

_____ dollars.

4. A package of daisy seeds costs $2. A box of tulip bulbs costs $19. How much do the seeds and the bulbs cost all together?

_____ dollars

Solve.

5. Gina plants 26 red and 17 yellow tulips. How many tulips does she plant in all?

_____ tulips

Kai plants 32 pink and 19 white tulips. How many tulips does he plant in all?

_____ tulips

How many tulips do Gina and Kai plant all together?

_____ tulips

6. Use the number sentence to write an addition story about a garden.

$48 + 18 = $ _____

_____

_____

_____

Rewrite Addition

 Write a number sentence to add.

1. There are 13 red fish. There are 5 silver fish. How many fish are there in all?

_____ fish in all

$13 + 5 =$ _____

   $+$ _____

2. There are 16 brown cats. There are 14 black cats. How many cats are there in all?

_____ cats in all

$16 + 14 =$ _____

   $+$ _____

 Write a number sentence to add.

3. Henry drew a picture of dogs. He drew 17 big and 15 small dogs. How many dogs did he draw in all?

_____ dogs in all

___ $+$ ___ $=$ ___

   $+$ _____

4. Meg collected 22 bird stickers. Her friend gave her 19 more. How many stickers does Meg have now?

_____ stickers

___ $+$ ___ $=$ ___

   $+$ _____

 **Solve. Use a separate sheet of paper to show your work.**

5. Kai has two books about butterflies. One book has 26 pictures. The other book has 38 pictures. How many pictures are there in all?

_____ pictures

6. Lily counts sheep to help her fall asleep. Last night she counted 48 sheep. Tonight she counted 39 sheep. How many sheep did Lily count in the two nights?

_____ sheep

Practice 2-Digit Addition

Solve.

1. Max sold 8 pet posters. Angie sold 21 pet posters. How many posters did Max and Angie sell in all?

   + ___

   _____ posters

2. This morning there were 16 people at the cat show. This afternoon there were 35. How many people were at the show today?

   + ___

   _____ people

Solve.

3. Greg bought two bags of dog biscuits for his dog. One bag has 46 biscuits. The other bag has 27. How many biscuits are there in all?

   + ___

   _____ biscuits

4. Tina walked her dog Rory for 33 minutes on Tuesday. She walked Rory for 49 minutes on Wednesday. How many minutes did they walk on both days?

   _____ minutes

   + ___

Solve.

5. Mr. Gumbel owns a pet shop. Someone wants to buy 80 fish. In one fish tank, he has 57 fish. In another fish tank, he has 42 fish. How many fish does he have in all?

   _____ fish

   Does he have enough fish? _____

   + ___

6. Buzz and Jo each have a sticker collection. Buzz has 36 stickers. Jo has 13 more than Buzz. How many stickers does Jo have?

   + ___

   _____ stickers

   Buzz has _____ stickers.

   Buzz and Jo together have _____ stickers.

   + ___

Solve. Check by adding in a different order.

1. There are 8 red ants at the picnic. There are 14 black ants. How many ants are there in all?

8 + 14 = ____ ants

14 + 8 = ____ ants

2. There were 12 bees in the rose garden. There were 23 bees in the tulip garden. How many bees were there in all?

12 + 23 = ____ bees

23 + 12 = ____ bees

 Solve. Check by adding in a different order.

3. Mai's bird chirped 24 times in one minute. Stan's bird chirped 37 times. How many times did the two birds chirp in all?

_____ times in all

$$\begin{array}{r} 24 \\ +37 \\ \hline \end{array}$$ $$\begin{array}{r} \\ + \\ \hline \end{array}$$

4. The frog hopped on 18 rocks. Then it hopped on 14 more. How many rocks did it hop on in all?

_____ rocks

$$\begin{array}{r} 18 \\ +14 \\ \hline \end{array}$$ $$\begin{array}{r} \\ + \\ \hline \end{array}$$

 **Solve. Check by adding in a different order.**

5. One farm has 26 cows and 18 horses. The second farm has 23 sheep and 19 pigs. How many animals are at both farms?

_____ animals

6. Lisa's dog does 14 tricks. Ben's dog does 9 tricks more than Lisa's dog. Ann's dog does 5 more than Ben's dog. How many tricks do the 3 dogs do in all?

_____ tricks

14.4

Estimate Sums

Round each number to the nearest 10. Circle the best estimate.

1. Sam's puppy has 11 spots. Mo's puppy has 18 spots. About how many spots do they have in all?

$10 + 10 = 20$ $10 + 20 = 30$

2. There were 16 black birds on the fence. There were 28 white birds. About how many birds were on the fence?

$10 + 20 = 30$ $20 + 30 = 50$

Estimate to solve. Use the number line above to help you round.

3. There are 34 cans of cat food. There are 38 cans of dog food. About how many cans in all?

about _____ cans

4. The toy store has 47 toy monkeys on the shelf. There are 36 more in back. About how many toy monkeys does the store have in all?

about _____ toy monkeys

 Estimate to solve. Use the number line above to help you round.

5. A movie about elephants is 43 minutes long. A movie about lions is 56 minutes long. How long are both movies together?

_____ minutes

nearest ten
+ ___   nearest ten   + ___

6. Jackie has a box of animal crackers. There are 45 elephant crackers and 52 tiger crackers in her box. How many tigers and elephants in Jackie's box?

nearest ten
+ ___   nearest ten   + ___

© Macmillan/McGraw-Hill

Add Three Numbers

 Add.

1. The zoo was open for 10 hours on Friday, 12 hours on Saturday, and 8 hours on Sunday. How many hours was it open those 3 days?

_____ hours

2. The bear took three naps. The first was 15 minutes long. The second was 23 minutes long. The third was 25 minutes long. How long did the bear nap in all?

_____ minutes

Use the table to answer the questions. Add.

Carrots Eaten			
Rabbit	April	May	June
Fuzzy	23	26	24
Fluffy	22	25	32

3. How many carrots did Fuzzy eat in all?

_____ carrots

4. How many carrots did Fluffy eat in all?

_____ carrots

 **Solve.**

5. Dr. Shu is an animal doctor. Last week she treated 24 cats, 36 dogs, and 12 birds. How many animals did she treat in all?

_____ animals

6. Dr. Shu also treats farm animals. Last month, she treated 35 horses, 15 goats and 12 pigs. How many farm animals did she treat in all?

_____ farm animals

Problem Solving: Strategy
Choose a Method

 **Choose a method to solve each problem. Then add.**

1. Abe has 8 stuffed animals. Annie has 20. How many do they have together?

_____ animals

2. Chip's bird says 12 words. If Chip teaches it 8 more, how many words will the bird say?

_____ words

 **Choose a method to solve each problem. Then add.**

3. Britt and Leslie drew pictures of ladybugs. Britt drew 34. Leslie drew 26. How many did they draw in all?

_____ ladybugs

4. A squirrel stored 23 nuts. A second squirrel stored 41 nuts. A third squirrel stored 34 nuts. How many nuts did they store in all?

_____ nuts

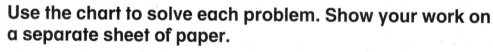 **Use the chart to solve each problem. Show your work on a separate sheet of paper.**

Number of Pets Sold			
Pet	January	February	March
turtles	15	22	19
fish	12	28	21
birds	5	15	13

5. In which month did the pet shop sell the most pets?

_____

6. Which kind of pet did the shop sell the most of in the three months?

_____

Subtract Tens

Write a subtraction sentence to solve.

1. What fact can help you subtract 40 − 30?

_____ − _____ = _____

2. What fact can help you subtract 80 − 60?

_____ − _____ = _____

Draw or write to solve.

3. The party is 90 minutes long. The friends spend 70 minutes bowling. How much time is left for eating cake and opening presents? _____ minutes

4. The second grade has 60 minutes at lunchtime. They spend the first 20 minutes eating lunch. How much time is left to play? _____ minutes

Write a subtraction sentence to solve.

5. Kyria has 8 dimes. She uses 2 dimes to buy milk. How much money does she have left?

_____ ¢ − _____ ¢ = _____ ¢

6. Alex shows 7 tens. He takes away 3 tens. How many tens does he have left?

_____ − _____ = _____

Count Back Tens and Ones to Subtract

 Write a subtraction sentence to solve.

1. How much is 52 − 2?

_____ − _____ = _____

2. How much is 86 − 20?

_____ − _____ = _____

 Write a subtraction sentence to solve.

3. There are 23 children in Ms. Va's class. 2 children are out sick. How many children are in class today?

_____ − _____ = _____

4. 49 people line up for the roller coaster ride. The gate opens and 20 people go in. How many people are left in the line?

_____ − _____ = _____

 **Use a simpler problem to solve.**

5. How many tens do you count back to subtract 81 − 30?

_____ tens

What is the difference?

_____

6. How many tens do you count back to subtract 48 − 10?

_____ tens

What is the difference?

_____

Decide When to Regroup

Use a picture to solve.

1. Subtract 3.

How many are left? _____

2. Subtract 7.

How many are left? _____

Draw a picture to solve.

3. Draw 53 in tens and ones. Subtract 4. How many are left? _____

4. Draw 28 in tens and ones. Subtract 9. How many are left? _____

Solve a 2-step problem. Draw or write to explain.

5. Erin has 6 tens 4 ones. She has to subtract 6. Does she need to regroup? _____

How many are left? _____

6. Chris has 2 tens 6 ones. He has to subtract 5. Does he need to regroup? _____ How many are left? _____

Subtract a 1-Digit Number
from a 2-Digit Number

Draw a picture to solve.

1. Sam has 15 crackers. He eats 8. How many are left?
_____crackers

2. Lisa has 20 raisins. She eats 9. How many are left?
_____ raisins

Solve.

3. Jessie has 34 points. During his turn he loses 7 points. How many points does he have now?
_____ points

4. Julia has 24 cards. She trades 6 cards for a notebook. How many cards does she have left?
_____ cards

Use a picture to solve.

5. Rita wants to give Paul 5 markers. Does she have to open a box? _____
How many markers will Rita have left?
_____ markers

6. Juan wants to give Kim 5 crayons. Does he have to open a box? _____
How many crayons will Juan have left?
_____ crayons

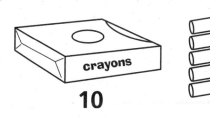

Subtract 2-Digit Numbers

Use the table to solve.

Month	Number of Days
August	31
February	28
April	30

1. How many more days are there in August than in February?

_____ more days

2. How many more days are there in April than in February?

_____ more days

Solve.

3. Raul has 56 animal stickers and 28 bird stickers. How many more animal stickers than bird stickers does he have?

_____ more bird stickers

4. Jake counts 23 cars and 7 trucks in his collection. How many more cars than trucks does he count?

_____ more cars

Cross out the extra information. Then draw or write to solve.

5. Vera has 21 stamps. Two of the stamps are the same. Meg has 9 stamps. How many more stamps does Vera have than Meg?

_____ more stamps

6. John has 15 points. Len has 6 points. David has 8 points. How many more points does John have than Len?

_____ more points

Solve.

1. 55 boys and 36 girls play soccer. How many more boys than girls is this?

_____ more boys

2. 88 girls dance. 23 girls take piano. How many more girls dance than take piano?

_____ more girls dance

Use the table to solve.

Class	Number of Students
Kindergarten	38
First grade	55
Second grade	62

3. How many more students are in second grade than kindergarten?

_____ more students

4. How many more students are in second grade than in first grade?

_____ more students

Cross out the extra information. Then solve.

5. There are 90 books in the classroom library. 45 of the books are fiction. Some of these books are easy readers. The rest of the books are non-fiction. How many of the books are non-fiction?

_____ books

6. There are 84 poems in a book. Some of the poems are about school. 69 of the poems are not about school. All of the poems are by the same author. How many of the poems are about school?

_____ poems

Problem Solving: Reading for Math

Cole and his mom went to the fruit stand.

First they picked 48 berries. Next they chose 12 apples.

Then they picked 18 peaches.

They paid for the fruit and went home to make fruit salad.

1. What fruit did they pick last?

_____

2. How many apples did they choose?

_____ apples

3. What fruit did they pick most of?

_____

4. What did they pick first, the berries or the apples?

_____

5. How many more of the first fruit than the last fruit did they pick?

_____ more

6. How many more of the last fruit did they pick than the second?

_____ more

Write a subtraction sentence to solve.

1. 53 geese are at the pond. 22 fly away. How many geese are still at the pond?

_____ – _____ = _____

2. 77 seagulls are on the beach. 17 fly away. How many are still on the beach?

_____ – _____ = _____

Draw or write to solve.

3. Kelly needs to regroup to subtract 64 – 27. Rewrite the subtraction so she can regroup. What is the difference?

4. Jared needs to regroup to subtract 82 – 45. Rewrite the subtraction so he can regroup. What is the difference?

Use the graph to solve.

Ben and his brothers made a graph to show their weight.

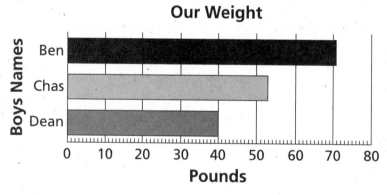

Our Weight

5. How many more pounds does Ben weigh than Chas?

_____ more pounds

6. How many more pounds does Ben weigh than Dean?

_____ more pounds

Practice 2-Digit Subtraction

 Draw or write to solve. Use a separate sheet of paper.

1. Amber has 50¢. She wants to buy a pencil for 99¢. How much more money does she need? _____ ¢

2. Eric has 25¢. He wants to buy an apple for 50¢. How much more money does he need? _____ ¢

Solve.

3. The low temperature was 45 degrees. The high temperature was 81 degrees. How many degrees did the temperature rise?

_____ degrees

4. Today's temperature was 47 degrees. Yesterday's temperature was 29 degrees. How many degrees warmer was it today than yesterday?

_____ degrees

Solve a 2-step problem.

5. Kia wants to read all 55 books by her favorite author. She has already read 20 of the chapter books and 7 of the easy readers. How many more books does she need to read?

_____ more books

6. Cody collects baseball team caps. He would like to get the caps for all 30 teams. He has caps for 10 teams in one league and 9 of the teams in the other. How many more caps does he need to collect?

_____ more caps

Check Subtraction

1. How can you add to check
38 − 12 = 26?

_____ + _____ = _____

2. How can you add to check
64 − 33 = 31?

_____ + _____ = _____

 **Use a pattern to solve.**

3. Complete the table.

60 − 20 = ___	40 + 20 = ___
60 − 19 = ___	41 + 19 = ___
60 − 18 = ___	42 + 18 = ___
60 − 17 = ___	43 + 17 = ___

4. Complete the table.

82 − 50 = ___	50 + 32 = ___
82 − 49 = ___	49 + 33 = ___
82 − 48 = ___	48 + 34 = ___
82 − 47 = ___	47 + 35 = ___

Solve a 2-step problem. Draw or write to explain. Use a separate sheet of paper.

5. Kelly buys milk for 25¢.
She pays with a half dollar.
She gets 20¢ change.
Is this correct? _____
How much change should
Kelly get? _____¢

6. Sam pays 24¢ for a 19¢
cup. The clerk gives him
5¢ change.
Is this correct? _____
How much change should
Sam get? _____

Estimate Differences

 Use a number line to estimate the difference. Circle the best estimate.

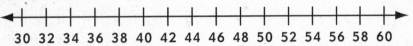

30 32 34 36 38 40 42 44 46 48 50 52 54 56 58 60

1. Maria counts 52 shells in the pail. She takes 31 out. About how many shells are left in the pail?

50 − 30 = 20   60 − 30 = 30

2. 58 children swim in the pool. Then 49 leave. About how many children stay in the pool?

50 − 50 = 0   60 − 50 = 10

 Rewrite the numbers to the nearest ten. Then subtract.

3. There are 72 boats docked. Then 27 boats leave for the race. About how many boats are still docked?

70 − _____ = _____

about _____ boats

4. 39 girls and 48 boys take sailing lessons. About how many more boys than girls take the lessons?

_____ − _____ = _____

about _____ more boys

 Rewrite the numbers to the nearest ten. Then subtract.

5. Lisa folds 60 paper birds in May. In August, she folds 77 paper birds. About how many more paper birds does she fold in August than in May?

about _____ more birds

6. The sled ride has 43 steps to the top. The tube ride has 72 steps. About how many more steps does the tube ride have than the sled ride?

about _____ more steps

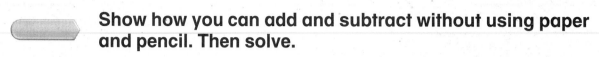

Show how you can add and subtract without using paper and pencil. Then solve.

1. Luke can add 27 + 21 without pencil and paper. What is the sum?

_____

2. Judi subtracts 74 − 22 without pencil and paper. What is the difference?

_____

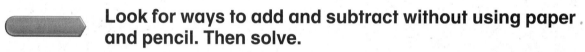

Look for ways to add and subtract without using paper and pencil. Then solve.

3. Asa has 41¢. Terry gives him 19¢ more. How much money does he have now?

_____¢

4. Niki has 68¢. She spends 52¢. How much money does she have left?

_____¢

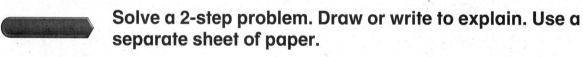

Solve a 2-step problem. Draw or write to explain. Use a separate sheet of paper.

5. Olga has 21 marbles. She gets 30 new marbles. Chris has 32 marbles. How many marbles do they have in all?

_____ marbles

6. Trevor has 29 baseball cards. Lori has 30 baseball cards. Then Lori gave 12 cards away. How many cards do they have in all?

_____ cards

Problem Solving: Strategy
Choose an Operation

Choose the operation to solve.

1. Jane has 15 rocks. Jake has 19. Do you add or subtract to find how many they have in all?

_____

2. There are 18 boys and 9 girls in the class. Do you add or subtract to find how many more boys than girls?

_____

Write a number sentence to solve.

3. 24 girls are waiting to jump rope. 18 leave for lunch. Do you add or subtract to find how many girls are still in line? _____

Write a number sentence.

___ ◯ ___ ◯ ___

How many girls are still in line? _____ girls

4. 22 boys play soccer and 15 boys play baseball. Do you add or subtract to find how many boys play all together? _____

Write a number sentence.

___ ◯ ___ ◯ ___

How many boys play all together? _____ boys

Cross out the extra information. Write a number sentence. Then solve.

5. The children make 29 snowmen. 21 have hats. 10 have carrot noses. Do you add or subtract to find how many snowmen do not have hats? _____

___ ◯ ___ ◯ ___

How many snowmen do not have hats? _____ snowmen

6. 28 girls and 33 boys sign up for soccer camp. All the children are 8 years old. Do you add or subtract to find how many children signed up in all? _____

___ ◯ ___ ◯ ___

How many children signed up in all? _____ children

Nonstandard Units of Length

Solve. Complete the number sentence.

1. A pencil is about 7 [o] long. A pen is about 9 [o] long. How much longer is the pen? 9 − 7 = _____ about _____ [o] longer

2. A crayon is about 6 [o] long. A paper clip is about 3 [o] long. How much shorter is the paper clip? 6 − 3 = _____ about _____ [o] shorter

Write a subtraction fact to explain your answer.

3. Jenny has a red stick and a blue stick. The red stick is about 12 [o] long. The blue stick is about 8 [o] long. About how much shorter is the blue stick?

_____ − _____ = _____ [o]

4. Tom has a white candle and a green candle. The white candle is about 13 [o] long. The green one is about 16 [o] long. About how much longer is the green candle?

_____ − _____ = _____ [o]

Solve.

5. George needs a box for his toy. The toy is 12 [o] high, 14 [o] wide, and 10 [o] long. Which box should he get?
Box A: 11 [o] high, 13 [o] wide, 10 [o] long
Box B: 13 [o] high, 15 [o] wide, 11 [o] long

6. A fork is 8 [o] long. A spoon is 6 [o] long. A knife is 9 [o] long. Write number sentences to compare lengths. Solve.

Measure to the Nearest Inch

Solve. Circle the correct answer.

1. A book is 12 inches long. A card is 6 inches long. How much shorter is the card?

8 inches   4 inches   6 inches

2. A flower is 8 inches long. A leaf is 3 inches long. How much longer is the flower?

4 inches   5 inches   11 inches

Write a number sentence to solve.

3. A pencil box is 10 inches long. A pencil is 7 inches long. How much longer is the pencil box than the pencil?

_____ inches longer

_____

4. One toy train is 3 inches long. How long is a chain of 2 toy trains?

_____ inches long

_____

Solve. Show your work.

5. A paper clip is 2 inches long. How many paper clips do you need to make a chain that is 8 inches long?

_____ clips

_____

6. Tony wants to frame a picture. His picture is 7 inches wide and 5 inches high. The frame should be 2 inches longer and 2 inches higher than the picture. How big will his frame be?

_____ inches wide and _____ inches high

_____

Inch, Foot, and Yard

 Circle the best answer.

1. About how long is a piece of chalk?

3 inches   3 feet   3 yards

2. About how long is a sheet of writing paper?

1 inch   1 foot   1 yard

 **Write a number sentence to solve.**

3. Ellen's scarf is 6 feet long. Jill's scarf is 2 feet shorter. How long is Jill's scarf?

_____ feet long

_____

4. A blue fence is 15 yards long. A red fence is 6 yards longer. How long is the red fence?   _____ yards long

_____

Solve. Show your work.

1 foot	=	12 inches
1 yard	=	3 feet

5. Marie has a stuffed giraffe. It is 3 feet high. How high is that in inches?

_____ inches

6. Jake made a banner that is 2 yards long. Ted made a banner that is 5 feet long. Whose banner is longer?

_____

How much longer is it?

_____

_____

Centimeter and Meter

Write a number sentence to solve.

I. A book is 13 centimeters long. A crayon is 7 centimeters long. How much longer is the book?

_____ centimeters longer

_____

2. A blue rug is 5 meters long. A pink rug is 2 meters long. How much shorter is the pink rug?

_____ meters shorter

_____

Solve. Then explain.

3. Which is longer, 90 centimeters or 1 meter?

_____

4. Jasper wants to measure the length of his shoe. Will he use a centimeter ruler or a meter stick?

_____

Solve. Then explain.

5. The distance from the table to the window is 120 centimeters. How much longer is that than a meter?

_____ centimeters longer

6. Karin has a piece of cloth that is 1 meter long. She wants to cut 2 pieces of cloth that are 50 centimeters long. Does she have enough cloth? _____

_____

© Macmillan/McGraw-Hill.

Problem Solving: Reading for Math

Solve. Show your work.

1. Rick's model dinosaur is 1 foot long. Alex's model dinosaur is 16 inches long. Whose model is longer?

_____

2. Danny drew a picture of 3 dinosaurs. They measure 1 foot long, 7 inches long, and 10 inches long. Write the lengths from shortest to longest.

_____

Solve.

3. Diana has two big posters. Her dinosaur poster is 1 yard long. Her poster of the planets is 45 inches long. Which poster is longer?

_____

4. Juan drew a big picture of 3 trees. His trees measure 11 inches, 13 inches, and 20 inches. Which trees are greater than 1 foot tall?

_____

Solve. Show your work.

5. The slide in the playground is 10 feet high. Is that longer or shorter than 3 yards? _____
How many feet longer or shorter? _____ feet

_____

6. The seesaw on the playground is 8 feet long. How much longer is it than 2 yards?

_____ feet longer

_____

Estimate to solve.

1. Which holds more dirt, a shovel, or a dump truck?

_____

2. Which holds less soup, a spoon or a bowl?

_____

 Solve.

3. Carrie is filling a fish tank. She can use a pot or a cup. Which holds more?

_____

4. Kevin fills a shovel with sand. Mark fills a pail with sand. Which holds less?

_____

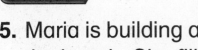

5. Maria is building a castle at the beach. She fills a cup with sand. She wants to use a container that can hold more than 1 cup. What could she use?

_____

6. Lou buys a small milk on Monday. He drinks it, but is still thirsty. He buys a large milk on Tuesday. He drinks it, then is not thirsty. Why?

_____

Solve.

1. Brian drinks 1 cup of water. Nate drinks 1 pint of water. Who drinks more?

   _____

2. Does a juice box you drink for lunch hold more than 1 quart or less than 1 quart?

   _____

Solve.

3. Mr. Park uses 1 pint of milk to make oatmeal. He uses 1 cup of milk to make pancakes. Which breakfast food uses less milk?

   _____

4. Does a pool hold more than 1 gallon or less than 1 gallon of water? Estimate.

   _____

Solve.

5. Ms. Levi goes to the store to buy 1 gallon of milk. The store has only quarts on the shelf. How many quarts should Ms. Levi buy so that she has the same amount of milk as in 1 gallon?
   _____ quarts

6. The doctor tells Kate to drink 1 pint of water with each meal. She drinks 1 cup of water at lunch. How much more water should she drink to follow the doctor's orders?

   _____

Ounce and Pound

 Use estimation to solve.

1. What is a good estimate? Circle.

more than 1 ounce
less than 1 ounce

2. What is a good estimate? Circle.

more than 1 pound
less than 1 pound

 Use estimation to solve.

3. Lori weighs her math book. Is it closer to 1 ounce or 1 pound?

_____

4. Does a page from your math book weigh less than 1 ounce or more than 1 ounce?

_____

 **Solve.**

5. Frank estimates that a plant weighs less than 1 pound. He places a 1-pound weight on one pan of a balance scale. He puts the plant on the other pan. The pan with the plant goes down. Was Frank's estimate correct? _____

6. Jill puts a 1-pound weight on a pan of a balance scale. How many ounces will balance the scale?
_____ ounces

 **Solve.**

I. Ann fills her spoon with milk. Is it more or less than I milliliter?

_____

2. Does a mug hold more or less than I liter?

_____

 **Draw a picture to solve. Use a separate sheet of paper.**

3. Ana's pail holds more than I liter. What else holds more than I liter?

_____

4. The dog bowl holds less than I liter. What else can hold less than I liter?

_____

 **Solve. One gallon is about 4 liters.**

5. Jon fills a 2-gallon container with water. Does it hold more than 6 liters or less than 6 liters?

6. Pari's fish tank holds about 20 liters. She needs to empty the water to clean it. Can she hold the water in a 3-gallon bucket or does she need to use the tub?

© Macmillan/McGraw-Hill.

_____   _____

Gram and Kilogram

 Use estimation to solve.

1. What is a good estimate? Circle.

lighter than 1 kilogram
heavier than 1 kilogram

2. What is a good estimate? Circle.

lighter than 1 kilogram
heavier than 1 kilogram

 Use estimation to solve.

3. Lori puts her full backpack on a scale. Is it lighter or heavier than 1 kilogram?

_____

4. Does a page from Lori's homework folder weigh less than 1 kilogram or more than 1 kilogram?

_____

 **Use estimation to solve.**

5. Cato puts a pair of shoes on the scale. Together the shoes weigh about 1 kilogram. About how much does 1 of the shoes weigh?

_____

6. Asha measures mass in grams. Asha has a bag of grapes with a mass of 100 grams. Is this more or less than 1 kilogram? Circle the answer.

less than 1 kilogram

more than 1 kilogram

Color to show the answer.

1. Show 30°F.

2. Show 18°C.

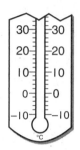

 Solve.

3. Erin looks out the window and sees snow falling. What might the temperature be in degrees Fahrenheit?

_____

4. On a hot day a thermometer reads 27 degrees. Is it measuring degrees in Fahrenheit or Celsius?

_____

 **Solve.**

5. When Pao went to school, the temperature was 47°F. When he left, the temperature was 39°F. Did the temperature get warmer or colder?

_____

6. Luke's job is to read the thermometer. He sees that the mercury stops between 54° and 56°F. What is the temperature?

_____

© Macmillan/McGraw-Hill.

Problem Solving: Strategy
Use Logical Reasoning

 Write your answer.

1. What tool can tell you how heavy a rock is?

_____

2. What tool can tell you how long a table is?

_____

 Solve. Write your answer.

3. Chrissy wants to see whether peanuts weigh more or less than 1 pound. What tool can she use?

_____

4. Ryan needs to measure the amount of water a watering can holds. What tool can he use?

_____

 Solve. Write your answer.

5. Lynn wakes up and sees snow on the ground. She wants to know how cold it is outside. What tool does she need?

_____

She wants to know how deep the snow is. What tool does she need?

_____

6. Jim needs 1 pound of peaches to make a pie. What tool does he need to weigh the peaches?

_____

He also needs to measure some sugar. What tool might he use?

_____

3-Dimensional Figures

rectangular prism   cone   cylinder   sphere   pyramid

 Solve.

1. Which 3-dimensional figure has 2 faces?

_____

2. Which 3-dimensional figure has 1 face?

_____

 Solve.

3. Taylor is on a ball field. He finds an object in the shape of a sphere. Is it a soccer ball or a football?

_____

4. David is at a party. Ms. Cruz gives him an object in the shape of a cylinder. Is it a party hat or a can?

_____

 **Draw a picture to solve the riddles.**

5. I am a cylinder. One of my faces is missing. You can put flowers in me. What am I?

_____

6. I am a rectangular prism. One of my faces has an opening. You need me when you sneeze. What am I?

_____

2-Dimensional Shapes

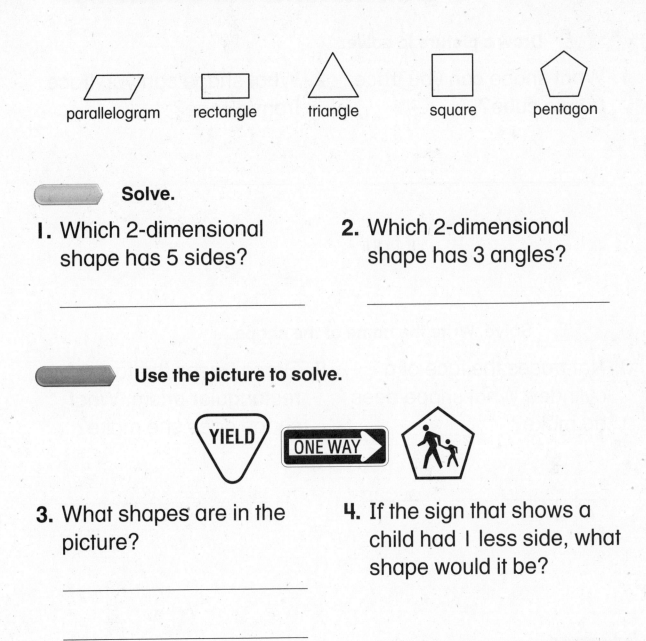

parallelogram   rectangle   triangle   square   pentagon

Solve.

1. Which 2-dimensional shape has 5 sides?

_____

2. Which 2-dimensional shape has 3 angles?

_____

Use the picture to solve.

3. What shapes are in the picture?

_____

_____

4. If the sign that shows a child had 1 less side, what shape would it be?

_____

Solve.

5. Kayla can draw 3 different quadrilaterals. What are their names?

_____

6. Omar draws 1 line to make a shape. It has no angles. What is the shape?

_____

© Macmillan/McGraw-Hill.

2-Dimensional and 3-Dimensional Relationships

Draw a picture to solve.

1. What shape can you trace from a cube?

_____

2. What shape can you trace from a cone?

_____

Solve. Write the name of the shape.

3. Nat traces the face of a cylinder. What shape does he make?

_____

4. Grace traces the face of a rectangular prism. What shape does she make?

_____

Solve. Write the name of the shape.

5. Emily wants to draw a square. She traces the face of a 3-dimensional figure to make one. What figure does she use?

_____

6. Zack wants to draw a circle. He traces the face of a 3-dimensional figure to make one. What figure does he use?

_____

Combine Shapes

 Draw a picture to solve.

1. Put 2 triangles together. What shape do you make?

_____

2. Put 2 squares together. What shape do you make?

_____

 Solve. Write the name of the shape.

3. Nick makes a hexagon with 2 pattern blocks of the same shape. What shape blocks does he use?

_____

4. Rachel makes a trapezoid with 3 pattern blocks of the same shape. What shape blocks does she use?

_____

 **Solve. Write the number and the name of the shape.**

5. Frank uses 4 shapes to make a hexagon. Some of the shapes are alike. Some are different. What shapes does he use?

_____

6. Olivia says she knows 2 different ways to make a hexagon with pattern block shapes. What blocks can she use?

_____

© Macmillan/McGraw-Hill.

Shape Patterns

 **Find a pattern to solve.**

1. Bob makes a pattern. What shape comes next?

_____

2. Ali makes a pattern. What shape comes next?

_____

 Find the pattern that repeats.

3. Justin makes a letter pattern. Which part of his pattern repeats?

A B C A B C A B C A B C

_____

4. Erica makes a fun pattern. Which part of her pattern repeats?

+ + > > + + > > + + > >

_____

 **Use a picture to solve. Use a separate sheet of paper.**

5. Draw a pattern that uses 3 shapes. What part of the pattern repeats? Circle it.

6. Draw a pattern that uses 4 shapes. What part of the pattern repeats? Circle it.

Problem Solving: Reading for Math

Cassie drew this picture.

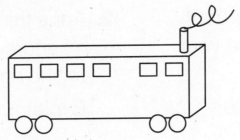

 Use the picture to solve.

1. How many circles?
_____ circles

2. Color the cylinder red.

 **Use the picture above to solve.**

3. Cassie wants to paint the circles black. How many circles will she paint black?
_____ circles

4. What 3-dimensional figure is the train car?

_____

Use the picture above to solve.

5. Write your own question about Cassie's picture. Make sure your question can be answered with the name of a 2-dimensional shape.

_____

_____

6. Think of another figure or shape that you would put in Cassie's drawing. Name the figure or shape.

_____

Solve.

1. What does congruent mean? Underline your answer.

4 sides and 4 angles

different shapes

same size and shape

flip and turn

2. Anne thinks that a circle and a square can be congruent. Is she right? _____

Explain.

_____

Solve.

3. Circle the 2 shapes that are congruent.

_____

4. Are the 2 circles congruent?

_____

Draw a picture to solve.

5. Eva wants to draw a flower with triangles for petals. The triangles are not congruent. Draw 2 triangles that she might use.

6. Mr. Ritter buys two square frames. They are congruent. Draw what the frames might look like.

Symmetry

 Solve.

1. Vito folds a square of paper in half. Did he make a line of symmetry?

_____

2. Ian draws a shape. It has many lines of symmetry. What shape is it?

_____

 Draw a picture to solve.

3. Van drew the block letter C. How many lines of symmetry does the C have?

_____ line of symmetry

4. Kit drew the block letter H. How many lines of symmetry does the H have?

_____ lines of symmetry

 **Solve the riddle. Then complete the picture.**

5. You color me red on Valentine's Day. I have one line of symmetry. What am I?

6. Birds make nests in me. You color me green. I may have one line of symmetry. I may have no lines of symmetry. What am I?

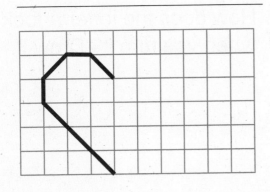

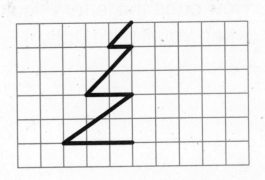

Slides, Flips, and Turns

 Use the picture to solve.

1. Laura moves a triangle. Did she flip it or turn it?

_____

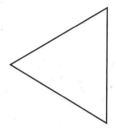 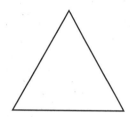

2. Simon moves his triangle. Did he slide it or flip it?

_____

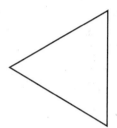 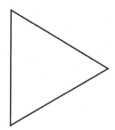

 **Solve.**

3. Luz slides the trapezoid block to Chris. Is sliding the block the same as turning it?

_____

4. Ana flips the trapezoid block. Is the block still facing the same way?

_____

Draw a picture to solve.

5. How does the letter F look when you flip it? Draw it.

6. How does the letter A look when you turn it? Draw it.

Perimeter

Solve.

1. Matt wants to find the perimeter of his shape.

2 cm
1 cm   1 cm
2 cm

What is the perimeter?

____ + ____ + ____ + ____ = ____ centimeters

2. Katia wants to find the perimeter of her table top.

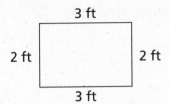

3 ft
2 ft   2 ft
3 ft

What is the perimeter?

____ + ____ + ____ + ____ = ____ feet

Draw a picture to solve. Use a separate sheet of paper.

3. Ms. Lopez has a garden. Two of the sides are 4 feet long. The other two sides are 5 feet long. What is the perimeter of the garden? _____ feet

4. Cody draws a square. Each side is 3 cm long. What is the perimeter of the square? _____ cm

Solve a 2-step problem.

5. Kiesha draws a shape. Two of the sides are 3 inches long. The other two sides are 1 inch long. What shape does Kiesha draw?

_____

What is the perimeter? _____ inches

6. Dan measures each side of a shape to find the perimeter. He finds the perimeter to be 3 inches. What might the shape be?

_____

How many inches long is each side? _____ inch

Area

Use the picture to solve.

1. Andy draws this grid of the soccer field. How many square units is it?

_____

2. Jamie measures her yard. What is the area?

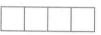

_____

Solve.

3. Marc uses 7 pattern block squares to cover a block letter T. What is the area of the T?

_____ square units

4. Hannah made a patio with 10 square concrete stones. What is the area of her patio?

_____ square units

Draw a picture to solve.

5. Melinda says the area of her shape is 4 square units. Draw a picture of her shape.

6. Tim uses 2 rows of 4 block square units to measure the area of a design. What is the area?

_____ square units

Draw a picture to show the area of Tim's design.

Problem Solving: Strategy
Guess and Check

Use guess and check to solve.

1. The perimeter of a square is 8 cm. How long is each side? _____ cm

2. The perimeter of a square is 20 cm. How long is each side? _____ cm

Use guess and check to solve.

3. Jose made a square sign. The perimeter is 24 inches. How long is each side? _____ inches

4. Chloe bought a square poster. The perimeter is 32 inches. How long is each side? _____ inches

Use guess and check to solve. Draw or write to explain.

5. Jordan measures the perimeter of a square piece of fabric. She needs 28 inches of lace to trim it. How long is each side of the square?

   _____ inches

6. Seth draws a rectangle. The perimeter is 14 cm. How long is each side of the rectangle?

   _____

Hundreds

 Use a picture to solve.

1. What number does Brian show?

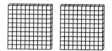

_____

2. What number does Kyle show?

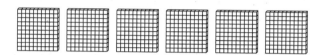

_____

 Solve.

3. How many people are in the park? Rao guessed 10 tens. How many people is that?

_____ people

4. How many fish are in the lake? Leah guessed 700 ones. How many fish is that?

_____ fish

 Solve. Show your work.

5. Joel has a roll of 50 dimes. He goes to the bank and trades the dimes for dollar bills. How many dollars does he get?

_____ dollars

6. Kali has 3 dollars but he needs dimes. He trades the dollars for dimes. How many dimes does he get?

_____ dimes

Hundreds, Tens, and Ones

Solve.

1. The doughnut shop made 576 doughnuts. How many hundreds? _____

   How many tens? _____

   How many ones? _____

2. There are 390 dogs at the dog show. How many hundreds? _____

   How many tens? _____

   How many ones? _____

Solve.

3. Val uses blocks to show the number 283. What blocks does she use?

   ___ hundreds
   ___ tens ___ ones

4. Bill uses blocks to show the number 148. What blocks does he use?

   ___ hundred
   ___ tens ___ ones

Solve.

5. Pete brings 100 crayons to school. His teacher has a box of 24 crayons. If they put the crayons together, what number will they show?

   _____ crayons

6. There are 180 days of school this year. Today is the hundredth day of school. How many more days of school are there this year?

   _____ more days

Place Value Through Hundreds

Use a picture to solve.

1. What is the value of the
1 in the number 214?

_____

2. What is the value of the
4 in 457?

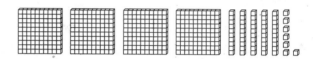

_____

Write a number sentence to solve.

3. Jose shows 8 hundreds,
3 tens, and 9 ones. What
number does he show?

_____ + _____ + _____

= _____

4. Deb shows 7 hundreds,
6 tens, and 1 one. What
number does she show?

_____ + _____ + _____

= _____

Solve.

5. Ms. Green is thinking of a
number. The value of the
ones digit is 5. The value of
the tens digit is 0. The
value of the hundreds digit
is 900. What is the
number?

_____

6. Mr. Ruiz asks the class to
guess a number. The
number can be written as
0 + 40 + 600. What is the
number?

_____

Explore Place Value to Thousands

 Use a picture to solve.

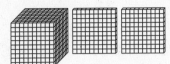

1. How many thousands are shown above?

_____ thousand(s)

2. What number do the blocks show?

_____

 Solve.

3. How can Mira write 1 thousand, 4 hundreds, 3 tens, and 8 ones?

___ + ___ + ___ + ___

_____

4. Dave counts by thousands. What numbers come next?

1,000, 2,000, ____, ____, ____

 **Solve.**

5. Mario wanted to write the number 2,901. He wrote 2000 + 900 + 10 + 1. Is this right? If not, make it right.

___ + ___ + ___ + ___

_____

6. Use the digits 1, 2, 3, and 4. How can you make a number that is more than 2,000 but less than 3,000?

_____

Problem Solving: Reading for Math

 Solve.

Stamp Collectors

Nina and Dave collect stamps. Nina has 205 stamps. Dave has 137 stamps. 100 of Dave's are from the USA. The rest are from other countries.

1. Who has more stamps?

_____

2. How many of Dave's stamps are from the USA?

_____ stamps

 Solve.

3. What is the main idea of the story?

_____

4. How many hundreds, tens, and ones are in 205?

___ hundreds ___ tens ___ ones

 **Solve.**

5. How many of Dave's stamps are from other countries?

_____ stamps

6. Nina's grandmother gave her 10 stamps from Italy. How many stamps does Nina have now?

_____ stamps

Solve.

1. What is different about these two numbers?

   789 and 779

   _____

2. Compare. Write > or <.

   678 ◯ 782

   542 ◯ 306

   128 ◯ 465

   854 ◯ 158

Write the following numbers. Then compare. Write < or > .

3. Benji has 223 marbles. Steve has 530 marbles.

   223 ◯ 530

   Who has the greater number of marbles?

   _____

4. Farmer Don has 712 corn stalks. He has 312 tomato plants.

   712 ◯ 312

   Does he have more corn stalks or tomato plants?

   _____

Solve.

5. Seth saved 347 bottle caps. Jorge saved 345. Who saved the greater number of caps?

   _____

6. Brett can buy a video game for $299. The regular price is $100 more. Is the regular price **greater than** or **less than** $400?

   _____

   Explain.

   _____

Order Numbers on a Number Line

Solve.

1. Write the number that is just before or just after.

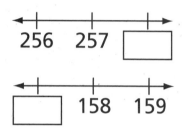

256   257   ☐

☐   158   159

2. Write the number that is between.

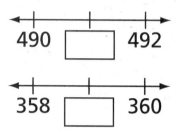

490   ☐   492

358   ☐   360

Solve.

3. The hotel room key has the number 465 written on it. What room number comes after that?

_____

4. Uncle Joe bought three raffle tickets. The tickets are numbered in order. One ticket has the number 167 on it. One ticket says 169. What number is on the other ticket?

_____

 **Solve.**

5. Dad signed up for a big race. He was given the number 765. What number does the person right before him have?

_____

6. I am between these numbers: 7 hundreds, 2 tens, and 1 one and 7 hundreds, 1 ten, and 9 ones. What number am I?

_____

Order Numbers

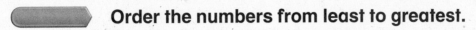 **Order the numbers from least to greatest.**

1. 346, 236, 564, 124

2. 786, 789, 897, 768

____ , ____ , ____ , ____

____ , ____ , ____ , ____

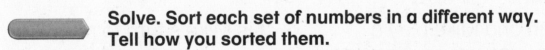 **Solve.**

3. Some classrooms at the school have these numbers: Class 207, Class 211, Class 243, and Class 208. Order them from least to greatest.

4. The students were playing a number game. Tess picked 483. Jamie picked 492 and Sadie picked 439. Jenny picked 432. Order the numbers from greatest to least.

____ , ____ , ____ , ____

____ , ____ , ____ , ____

Solve. Sort each set of numbers in a different way. Tell how you sorted them.

5. 456, 246, 386, 256, 476

6. 545, 690, 780, 237, 312

____ , ____ , ____ , ____ , ____

____ , ____ , ____ , ____ , ____

How did you sort the numbers?

How did you sort the numbers?

_____

_____

Number Patterns

Solve.

1. Jody is counting out loud: 511, 512, 513, 514, 515, 516. What counting pattern is Jody using?

_____

2. Phil likes to doodle. He wrote the following numbers on the cover of his notebook: 236, 246, _____, 266, _____, 286. Fill in the missing numbers. Name the pattern.

_____

Solve.

3. Paul counted by hundreds. He started with the number 123. Write the numbers Paul counted.

123 ___ ___ ___ ___ ___

4. Alli counted by tens. She started with the number 325. Write the numbers that Alli counted.

325 ___ ___ ___ ___ ___

Solve. Name the counting pattern.

5. Shari and Mike play a game. Shari counted: 129, 139, 149, 159, 169. Shari wants Mike to guess her counting pattern. What should Mike guess?

_____

6. It is Mike's turn to play. He counted: 125, 140, 130, 135, 120, 145. Put Mike's numbers in order from least to greatest.

___ ___ ___ ___ ___

Guess the counting pattern. Counting by _____

Count Forward, Count Backward

 Solve.

1. Jen counted forward by tens. Write the missing numbers.

276 ____ ____

736 ____ ____

2. Brett counted backward by ones. Write the missing numbers.

985 ____ ____

246 ____ ____

 **Solve.**

3. Sandi read a funny story about a dog that liked to count. The dog said, "400, 300, 200." How did the dog count?

_____

4. The dog said he had lots of cousins. Then he counted them, "201, 202, 203," and so on. How did the dog count?

_____

Write the number.

5. I am 10 less than 258. What number am I?

_____

Add 100 to that number. Now what number am I?

_____

6. I am 1 ten and 5 ones more than 50. What number am I?

_____

Count backward by 2 tens. What number am I?

_____

© Macmillan/McGraw-Hill.

Problem Solving: Strategy
Make a Table

 Complete the table to solve.

Liz calls her 2 grandmothers every week.

Weeks	1	2	3	4	5
Calls	2	4	6	__	__

1. How many calls does Liz make in 4 weeks?

_____ calls

2. How many calls does Liz make in 5 weeks?

_____ calls

 Complete the table to solve.

Mrs. Jones gives 3 jars of paint to each group. There are 5 groups in the class.

Group	1	2	3	4	5
Paints	3	__	__	12	__

3. Groups 1 and 2 share one art table. How many jars of paint are on their table?

_____ jars

4. How many jars of paint are there in all? _____ jars

Complete the table to solve.

Mr. Frank's class collected cans for a recycling project. They collected 100 cans each week for five weeks.

___	1	2	3	4	5

5. How many cans did they collect in all?

_____ cans

6. Look at the completed table. What's the counting pattern?

_____

How many cans will the class collect in 6 weeks?

_____ cans

© Macmillan/McGraw-Hill.

Add Hundreds

 **Solve.**

1. The fair came to town. There were 300 yellow balloons and 200 green balloons. How many balloons were there in all?

3 hundreds + 2 hundreds = ____ hundreds

300 + 200 = _____

2. There were 500 blue streamers and 200 orange streamers. How many streamers were there in all?

5 hundreds + 2 hundreds = ____ hundreds

500 + 200 = _____

Solve.

3. 200 girls and 200 boys went to the fair on Saturday. How many went on Saturday in all?

____ + ____ = ____ children

4. The fair sold 400 tickets on Saturday and 500 on Sunday. How many tickets were sold in all?

____ + ____ = ____ tickets

Use the chart to solve.

Fair Snack Stand Sales

Snack	Saturday	Sunday
Bags of popcorn	400	200
Bags of peanuts	300	400

5. How many bags of popcorn were sold in all?

_____ + _____ = _____

How many bags of peanuts were sold in all?

_____ + _____ = _____

6. Were there more bags of popcorn sold or more bags of peanuts sold?

_____

Regroup Ones

Use another sheet of paper to regroup ones. Then solve.

1. There are 127 blue flags and 133 white flags. How many flags are there all together?

_____ flags

2. The circus traveled 246 miles on Tuesday. It traveled 225 miles on Wednesday. How many miles did it travel on Tuesday and Wednesday?

_____ miles

Solve. Show your work.

3. The circus performed 247 days last year. It performed 235 days the year before. How many days did it perform in those two years?

_____ days

4. There are two tigers in the circus. One tiger weighs 206 pounds. The other tiger weighs 188 pounds. How much do they weigh together? _____ pounds

Solve.

5. The circus orders 348 pounds of hay from Farmer Green and 437 pounds of hay from Farmer Brown. How many pounds does the circus order in all?

_____ pounds

6. The circus spends 466 dollars on food, and 329 dollars on water. How much money does it spend on food and water? ____ dollars

Does it spend **more** or **less** than $800? _____

Regroup Tens

Solve. Show your work. Circle the answer.

1. What is 358 plus 251?

509   5,109   609

Hundreds	Tens	Ones
+		

2. What is 426 plus 392?

8,118   818   718

Hundreds	Tens	Ones
+		

Solve. Show your work.

3. At the circus, Marie bought a hot dog for 165 cents. She bought a soda for 150 cents. How many cents did she spend in all? ____ cents

Hundreds	Tens	Ones
+		

4. Fred bought a hamburger for 270 cents. He bought a milk shake for 155 cents. How many cents did he spend in all? _____ cents

Hundreds	Tens	Ones
+		

Solve.

5. Jake and Trevor saved money to go to the zoo. Jake has 462 pennies. Trevor has 386 pennies. How many pennies have they saved up? ____ pennies

6. Tickets are 4 dollars each. Do Jake and Trevor have enough money to go to the zoo? Explain.

_____

Problem Solving: Reading for Math

 Read and solve.

The theater is closed on Monday. There is one show a day from Tuesday through Friday. On Saturday and Sunday, there are two shows each day. The first show is in the afternoon. The second show is in the evening.

M	T	W	T	F	S	S
0	257	281	193	222	463	537

1. On which two days were the most tickets sold?

_____

Why were more tickets sold on those days?

_____

2. Why were there no ticket sales on Monday?

_____

 **Read and solve.**

3. How many tickets were sold on Tuesday and Wednesday?

_____ tickets

4. How many tickets were sold on Thursday and Friday?

_____ tickets

 Read and solve.

5. How many tickets were sold on Saturday and Sunday?

_____ tickets

6. Were more tickets sold from Tuesday to Friday, or on the weekend? Explain.

_____

Solve.

1. There are 300 balls. Take away 100 balls. How many balls are left?

3 hundreds – 1 hundred = _____ hundreds

300 – 100 = _____ left

2. There are 400 paper clips. Take away 200 paper clips. How many are left?

4 hundreds – 2 hundreds = _____ hundreds

400 – 200 = _____ left

 **Solve.**

3. Allison has 500 marbles. She gives Jimmy 300. How many marbles does Allison have left?

____ – ____ = ____ marbles

4. Paul has 600 baseball cards. He gives his brother 200. How many cards does Paul have left?

____ – ____ = ____ cards

Solve. Show your work.

5. Jim and Tad have 400 stickers. 200 of those stickers belong to Jim. How many belong to Tad?

_____ – _____ = _____

Does one boy have more stickers?

_____

6. Alicia has 900 pennies. She traded 500 pennies. How many pennies does she have left?

_____ – _____ = _____

How many dollar bills did she get for 500 pennies?

_____ bills

Regroup Tens as Ones

Solve.

1. Mr. Fino has a fruit stand. He had 245 apples. He sold 127 apples. How many apples are left? _____ apples

Hundreds	Tens	Ones
	☐	☐
2	4	5
− 1	2	7

2. There were 364 oranges. 155 oranges were sold. How many oranges are left? _____ oranges

Hundreds	Tens	Ones
	☐	☐
3	6	4
− 1	5	5

Solve. Show your work. Use a separate sheet of paper.

3. Ms. Florio's bakery had 254 cookies. She sold 127. How many cookies are left?

_____ cookies

4. There were 367 cakes. She sold 139 cakes. How many cakes are left?

_____ cakes

Solve. Show your work. Use a separate sheet of paper.

There were 465 roses on Monday. On Tuesday, 132 roses were sold. On Wednesday, 114 roses were sold. How many roses were left on Wednesday?

_____ roses left

5. Show how you can subtract two times to find the answer.

_____

_____

6. Show how you can use addition and subtraction to find the answer.

_____

_____

Regroup Hundreds as Tens

 **Solve.**

1. There were 339 paper cups. The class used 152. How many cups are left?

_____ cups

Hundreds	Tens	Ones
☐	☐	
3	3	9
− 1	5	2

2. There were 455 paper plates. The class used 263. How many plates are left?

_____ plates

Hundreds	Tens	Ones
☐	☐	
4	5	5
− 2	6	3

Solve. Show your work.

3. Mrs. Garza's trip is 457 miles long. She has already gone 274 miles. How many miles are left to go?

_____ miles

4. There are 368 children at the fair. 185 of them are boys. How many are girls?

_____ girls

Solve.

5. The Travel Club had 846 dollars. They went on a trip to the beach. A bus costs 450 dollars to rent. How much money did the club have left over?

_____ dollars

6. The Travel Club paid for snacks and drinks. Snacks cost 146 dollars. Drinks cost 163 dollars. How much money was left at the end of the trip?

_____ dollars

© Macmillan/McGraw-Hill.

Estimate, Add, and Subtract Money Amounts

Rewrite the amounts to the nearest dollar. Then add or subtract to solve.

1. A book costs $3.27. A magazine costs $2.85. About how much do they cost together?

   _____ + _____ = _____

   about _____

2. Harry has $7.38. He buys a pen for $3.76. About how much does he have left?

   _____ – _____ = _____

   about _____

Solve. Then estimate to see if your answer is reasonable.

3. Zoe has $8.25. She wants to buy a scarf for $5.85. How much money will she have left?

     $8.25 nearest dollar _____

   –$5.85 nearest dollar – _____

   _____

4. A hat costs $4.76. A pair of socks costs $3.42. How much do they cost together?

     $4.76 nearest dollar _____

   +$3.42 nearest dollar + _____

   _____

Solve. Show your work.

  $2.68

 $2.39

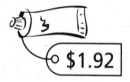 $1.92

5. Rewrite the amounts to the nearest dollar. About how much do the comb and toothbrush cost?

   about _____

   What is the real cost?

   _____

6. About how much do all three items cost? about

   _____

   You have $8.00. Will that be enough? _____

   What is the real cost?

   _____

Problem Solving: Strategy
Work Backward

 Solve.

1. The book is 246 pages long. Tess has already read 128 pages. How many pages are left to read?

```
  246
− 128
```
_____ pages left

2. Mr. Fix-It used 132 nails. There are 181 nails left in the box. How many nails were in the box?

```
  132
+ 181
```
_____ nails

 Solve. Draw or write to explain. Use a separate sheet of paper.

3. It is 748 miles from Davis to Blue Gorge. Ms. Peck has already driven 365 miles. How many more miles does she still have to drive?

_____ more miles

4. Al bought a birthday card for $1.75. He has $2.50 left. How much money did he have to begin with?

_____

Solve. Draw or write to explain. Use a separate sheet of paper.

5. Two classes are putting on a talent show. There are 500 tickets in all. One class sold 138 tickets. The other class sold 235. How many more tickets are left to sell?

_____ tickets

6. Anthony has $9.00. He wants to buy some presents. A game costs $3.75. A kite costs $5.34. A poster costs $4.25. Which two presents can he buy?

_____

Unit Fractions

Solve. Circle the drawing that shows the fraction.

1. Alan ate $\frac{1}{3}$ of a pizza.

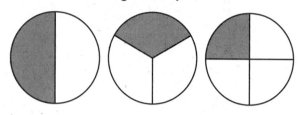

2. Lisa ate $\frac{1}{4}$ of a blueberry pie.

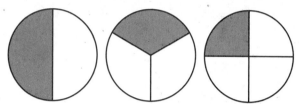

Solve. Write the fraction.

3. How much of the pizza did Frank eat?

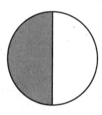

___ number of shaded parts
number of equal parts

4. How much of the pie did Genna eat?

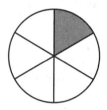

___ number of shaded parts
number of equal parts

Solve.

5. Look at each figure and its shaded part. Is anything the same? (Hint: What fraction does each show?)

  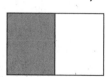

6. Sandy says she colored $\frac{2}{3}$ of the circle. Is she right? Explain.

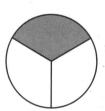

_____

_____

Fractions Equal to One

> **Solve.**

1.

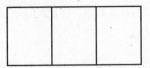

How many equal parts?

_____

What is the fraction for the whole? Circle it.

$\frac{2}{2}$ $\frac{3}{3}$ $\frac{5}{5}$

2.

How many equal parts?

_____

What is the fraction for the whole? _____

> **Solve.**

3. It is Drew's birthday. He cut his birthday cake into equal pieces. Circle the fraction for the whole.

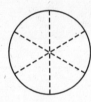

$\frac{3}{3}$ $\frac{6}{6}$ $\frac{8}{8}$

4. Dee cut a fruit tart into equal pieces. What is the fraction for the whole?

_____

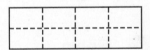

> **Solve.**

5. Jason baked a peach pie. He and 5 of his friends will eat it. Into how many equal pieces should he cut the pie? _____

What is the fraction for the whole? _____

6. Lin and Dave see two cookies. They will share one. Each cookie shows halves. Do you think Lin and Dave will pick cookie A or cookie B? Explain.

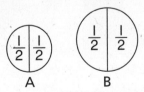

Solve.

1. How much of the chocolate cake was eaten at the party?

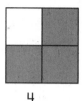

$\frac{2}{4}$ $\frac{3}{4}$ $\frac{4}{4}$

2. How much of the pizza was eaten?

$\frac{2}{6}$ $\frac{4}{6}$ $\frac{5}{6}$

Solve.

3. Grant ate $\frac{1}{3}$ of a veggie burger. Does this circle show the part that Grant ate? Explain.

4. Naomi's garden has 4 equal parts. She planted tomatoes and beans. She planted beans in only 1 part. What part of the garden did she plant tomatoes?

Solve.

5. Kali and James broke an orange into 5 parts. Kali ate $\frac{2}{5}$ of the orange. James ate $\frac{3}{5}$ of the orange. Label the picture that shows how much Kali ate. Label the picture that shows how much James ate.

Who ate more? _____

6. Paul cut a pizza into 6 equal sections. He ate 2 pieces. Put a **P** on each piece he ate. Amy ate $\frac{2}{6}$ of the pizza. Put an **A** on each piece she ate.

What fraction of the pizza did each person eat? _____

What fraction of the pizza is left? _____

Solve.

1.

1 of 3 equal parts is black. What fraction is black?

$\frac{1}{2}$ $\frac{1}{3}$ $\frac{1}{4}$

2.

3 of 5 equal parts is black. What fraction is black?

$\frac{1}{5}$ $\frac{2}{5}$ $\frac{3}{5}$

Solve.

3. Matt dropped 4 pennies. This picture shows how they landed.

What fraction of the group shows how many pennies landed heads up?

$\frac{1}{4}$ $\frac{2}{4}$ $\frac{3}{4}$

4. Matt drops 2 more pennies.

Now what fraction of the group shows heads?

_____

Solve. Show your work.

5. Jake has 5 balloons. $\frac{3}{5}$ of Jake's balloons are orange. Color the number of balloons that are orange.

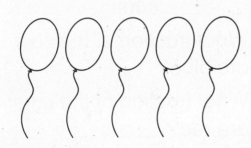

6. 6 birds are in a tree. Half of them fly away. How many birds are still in the tree?

_____ birds

Draw a picture to explain.

Solve.

1. Han has 4 marbles. 1 of the 4 marbles is blue. Which fraction shows the blue part?

$\frac{1}{4}$ $\frac{3}{4}$ $\frac{4}{4}$

2. Joey has 5 apples. 2 of the 5 apples are red. What fraction of the apples are red?

_____ are red.

Solve.

3.

What fraction of the fish are striped?

_____

4. Ginger gave $\frac{2}{5}$ of her shells to Howard. Shade the number of shells Ginger gave to Howard.

Solve. Draw pictures to explain.

5. Ingrid has 2 green bottles and 3 yellow bottles. How many does she have in all?
   _____ bottles
   What fraction of the bottles are green? _____

6. Steve has 4 red cars and 2 blue cars. How many cars does he have in all?
   _____ cars
   What fraction of the cars are blue? _____
   What fraction of the cars are red? _____

Compare Fractions

Solve.

1.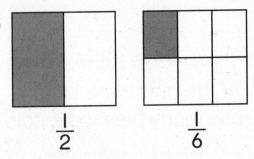

$\frac{1}{2}$ $\frac{1}{6}$

Compare the shaded parts. Which fraction is greater, $\frac{1}{2}$ or $\frac{1}{6}$? _____

2.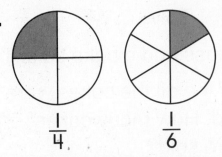

$\frac{1}{4}$ $\frac{1}{6}$

Compare the shaded part. Which fraction is less, $\frac{1}{4}$ or $\frac{1}{6}$? _____

Solve.

3. Al ate $\frac{1}{4}$ of a cookie. Ling ate $\frac{1}{3}$ of a cookie.

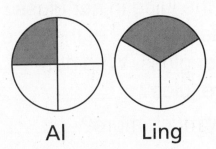

Al   Ling

Who ate more? _____

4. Ellen and Gil have 8 T-shirts each. $\frac{1}{2}$ of Ellen's T-shirts are white. $\frac{1}{4}$ of Gil's T-shirts are white. Who has more white T-shirts? Explain.

_____

_____

Solve.

5. Tom and Greg each order a cheese sandwich. Tom eats $\frac{1}{2}$ of his sandwich. Greg eats $\frac{1}{3}$ of his sandwich. Who eats more? Explain.

_____

6. There are 6 fish in a tank. $\frac{2}{6}$ of the fish are orange. There are 6 fish in a bowl. $\frac{3}{6}$ of the fish are orange. Does the tank or the bowl have more orange fish? Draw a picture.

_____

Problem Solving:
Reading for Math

Solve.

The class had a bake sale. There were 3 cakes and 5 pies.

1. $\frac{2}{3}$ of the all the cakes were sold. How many cakes were sold?

   _____ cakes sold

2. $\frac{4}{5}$ of the pies were sold. How many pies were sold?

   _____ pies sold

Solve.

Tina and Rose planted 10 tulip bulbs. They drank juice when they were done.

3. Each girl planted $\frac{1}{2}$ of the bulbs. How many bulbs did each girl plant?

   _____ bulbs

4. Tina and Rose shared a bottle of juice. Tina poured $\frac{2}{5}$ of the juice in her glass. Rose poured $\frac{3}{5}$ of the juice in her glass. Who had more juice? _____

   How much more? _____

Solve.

Daryl, Jim, Chuck, and Stan went camping. Chuck and Daryl put up the tent. Jim went into the woods to look for firewood.

5. What part of the group put up the tent? Write the fraction. _____

   What part of the group looked for firewood? Write the fraction. _____

6. Stan and Jim went fishing. They caught 5 fish. Stan caught 3 of them. Write the fraction of the fish Stan caught. _____

   Write the fraction of the fish Jim caught. _____

Explore Probability

 Solve.

1. Adam has a drawer of socks. All his socks are white. Is picking a white sock from the drawer probable or certain?

_____

2. Is picking a blue sock probable or impossible?

_____

 Solve. Write certain, probable, or impossible.

3. Matt has 6 marbles in his bag. 4 marbles are blue. 2 marbles are red. Picking a blue marble is

_____ .

4. Marie has 6 marbles in her bag. 1 marble is yellow. 6 marbles are black. Picking a blue marble is

_____ .

 **Solve.**

Chad has 5 green cubes, 5 blue cubes, and a bag.

5. Chad wants to make green the certain color to pick. What cubes would he put in the bag?

_____

6. Chad wants to make blue the probable color to pick. What cubes would he put in the bag?

_____

More Likely, Equally Likely, or Less Likely

Solve.

1. A bag has 1 penny and 5 dimes. Which coin are you more likely to pick?

_____

2. A bag has 4 pennies and 2 dimes. Which coin are you less likely to pick?

_____

Solve.

3. There are 7 cubes in a bag. 5 cubes are red. 2 cubes are orange. Which color are you more likely to pick?

_____

4. There are 6 cubes in a bag. 3 cubes are green. 3 cubes are blue. Are you more likely, less likely, or equally likely to pick blue?

_____

Solve.

5. There are 8 birds in a tree. They are crows or doves. You are equally likely to see a crow or a dove. How many crows are in the tree? _____

How many doves are in the tree? _____

Explain how you know.

_____

6. There are 4 black kittens and 4 orange kittens in a box. The owner says Sara and Nick must pick without looking. Sara picks an orange kitten. Is Nick more likely, less likely, or equally likely to get a black kitten?

_____

Explain how you know.

_____

Make Predictions

 Solve.

1. Ed's spinner has more red sections than blue ones. Predict what color he will land on more often.

red   blue

2. Sylvie has a cube. Four sides are orange. Two are green. Predict what color she will toss more often.

_____

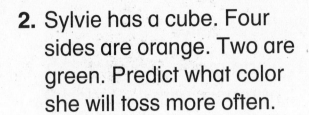 **Solve.**

3. Sal's spinner has 5 white sections. It has 1 black section. He spins. What color do you predict he will get? Explain. _____

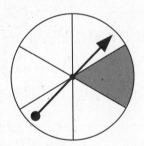

4. If Dana spins each of these spinners 10 times, which spinner will land on black most often? _____ Explain. _____

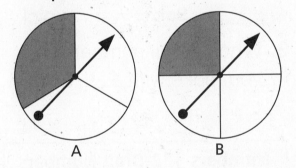

A   B

 **Solve.**

5. Laura's spinner has 3 green sections and 3 blue sections. She spins 12 times. Predict how many times the spinner will land on green and how many times it will land on blue. Explain.

_____

6. Erin has 8 marbles in a bag. 5 marbles are green. The rest are red. She pulls one marble out of the bag. Predict its color. Explain.

_____

Erin pulls out 3 marbles. They are all green. Predict the color of the next marble she pulls out. Explain.

Problem Solving: Strategy
Make a List

Solve.

1. Todd made 2-digit numbers with 1, 2, and 3. Finish what he started.

Numbers	2-Digit Numbers	
1	12	13
2	21	23
3		

2. Janet uses 3, 5, and 8. What 2-digit numbers can she make?

Numbers	2-Digit Numbers
3	35
5	53
8	85

Solve.

3. What 2-digit numbers can you make with 2, 4, and 7?

Numbers	2-Digit Numbers
2	
4	
7	

4. Frank made 2-digit numbers. Which 3 numbers did he use?

Numbers	2-Digit Numbers	
	34	39
	43	49
	93	94

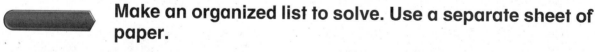

Make an organized list to solve. Use a separate sheet of paper.

5. Claire uses the numbers 3, 6, 8, and 9. What 2-digit numbers can she make?

6. Pick 3 different numbers. What 2-digit numbers can you make with them?

© Macmillan/McGraw-Hill.

Range and Mode

 Solve.

The bookstore sold this many mystery books in the last 4 days.

$$6 \qquad 10 \qquad 6 \qquad 9$$

1. What is the range of the numbers?

3   4   1

2. What is the mode of the numbers?

6   9   10

 **Solve.**

3. There are 5 kids in the Craft Club. Their ages are 8, 10, 8, 11, and 10 years old. What is the range of the numbers? _____

4. The table shows the number of books read. What is the mode of the numbers? _____

Name	Ann	Troy	Gary	Lee	Mia
Number of books	6	4	7	6	5

Solve. Show your work.

The table shows the number of children who brought apples to school last week.

Mon.	Tue.	Wed.	Thur.	Fri.
23	16	18	21	18

5. What is the range of the numbers? _____

6. What is the mode of the numbers? _____

Median

 Solve. Show your work.

1. Ollie worked these hours in the last 3 days.

$$4 \qquad 3 \qquad 5$$

Write the numbers in order:

_____

What is the median of the numbers? _____

2. Mr. Zip walked these miles in the last 4 days.

$$3 \qquad 2 \qquad 5 \qquad 1 \qquad 4$$

Write the numbers in order:

_____

What is the median of the numbers? _____

 Solve. Show your work.

The Pet Hospital treated this number of pets last week.

Mon.	Tue.	Wed.	Thur.	Fri.
4	6	3	7	9

3. What is the median of the numbers?

_____

4. Five of the pets are 5, 11, 9, 7, and 8 years old. What is the median age?

_____ years old

 **Solve. Show your work.**

Nan and Tilly's Lemonade Stand					
	Wed.	Thur.	Fri.	Sat.	Sun.
Cups of lemonade sold	8	10	14	15	16
Dollars collected	4	5	7	8	9

5. What is the median number of cups Nan and Tilly sold? _____

6. What is the median number of dollars they collected?

_____

Coordinate Graphs

The graph shows where animals are in the zoo.

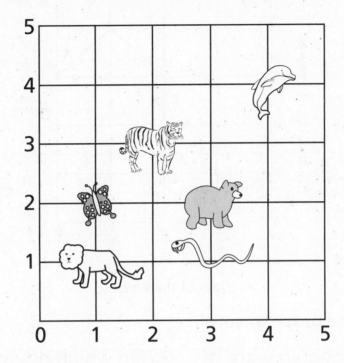

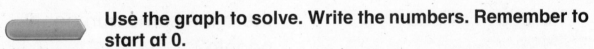

Use the graph to solve. Remember to start at 0.

1. Go right 1. Go up 1. What animal do you find?

_____

2. Go right 1. Go up 2. What animal do you find?

_____

Use the graph to solve. Write the numbers. Remember to start at 0.

3. How can you find the snake? Go right _____.
Go up _____.

4. How can you find the dolphin? Go right _____.
Go up _____.

Use the graph to solve.

5. What animal is up 1 from the snake? _____

What animal is right 2 from the butterfly? _____

6. Maria wants to find the tiger. She went right 3 and up 2. What mistake did Maria make? _____

Line Graphs

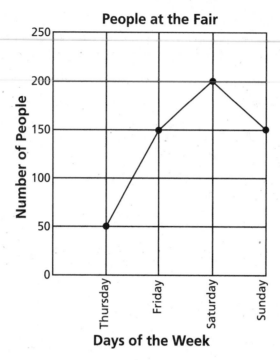

People at the Fair

Number of People

250
200
150
100
50
0

Thursday Friday Saturday Sunday

Days of the Week

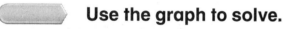

Use the graph to solve.

1. How many people were at the fair on Thursday?

_____

2. On which day were there the most people?

_____

Use the graph to solve.

3. Were there more people on Thursday or Friday?

_____

4. On which two days were there the same number of people?

_____

Solve. Show your work.

5. How many more people came on Saturday than on Thursday?

_____ more people

6. In order for the fair to make money, at least 500 people have to come in all. Did the fair make money? Explain.

_____

Problem Solving: Reading for Math

The Party Store just got in some boxes of supplies. Use the graph to answer the questions.

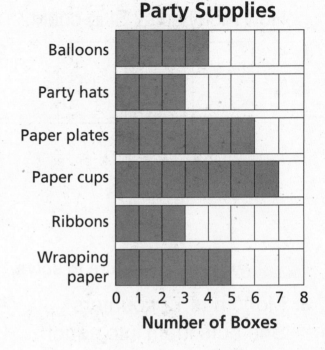

Party Supplies

Number of Boxes

 **Solve.**

1. How many boxes of paper plates were there?

   _____

2. How many boxes of wrapping paper were there? _____

 **Solve.**

3. Are there more boxes of balloons or wrapping paper?

   _____

4. Are there more boxes of party hats or ribbons?

   _____

 **Solve.**

5. How many more boxes of paper plates than party hats are there? _____

6. How many boxes did the store order in all?

   _____

   Tell how you know.

   _____

Explore Equal Groups

> **Solve.**

How many dots? Skip-count.

1.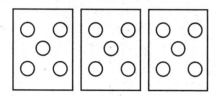

   _____ _____ _____

   _____ in all

2.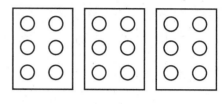

   _____ _____ _____

   _____ in all

> **Draw a picture to solve.**

3. Maria has 12 counters. She puts them into equal groups of 3. How many groups does she make?

   _____ groups of 3

4. Gary has 8 counters. He puts them into equal groups of 2. How many groups does he make?

   _____ groups of 2

>  **Solve. Draw a picture if you need help.**

5. Vic has 6 crackers. He wants to put the crackers into equal groups so he can share with friends. Circle all the equal groups that he can make.

   2   3   4   5

6. Lin has 12 grapes. She wants to put the grapes into equal groups so that she can share with friends. Circle all the equal groups that she can make.

   2   3   4   5   6

Repeated Addition and Multiplication

Write a number sentence to solve.

1. How many cubes?

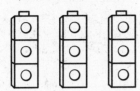

___ + ___ + ___ = ___

___ × ___ = ___

2. How many cubes?

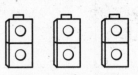

___ + ___ + ___ = ___

___ × ___ = ___

Write a number sentence to solve.

3. Lisa plays with 2 groups of marbles. Each group has 4 marbles. How many marbles does she use?

___ + ___ = ___

___ × ___ = ___

4. Brad makes 4 groups of cards. Each group has 3 cards. How many cards does he make?

___ + ___ + ___ + ___ = ___

___ × ___ = ___

Use a number sentence to solve.

5. Ms. White writes a number sentence.

$2 + 2 + 2 + 2 + 2 =$ _____

What is the sum? _____

What multiplication sentence can she write from the addition?

_____ × _____ = _____

6. Mr. Yun writes a number sentence.

$5 + 5 + 5 =$ _____

What is the sum? _____

What multiplication sentence can he write from the addition?

_____ × _____ = _____

© Macmillan/McGraw-Hill.

Use a picture to solve.

1. How many in all? Multiply.

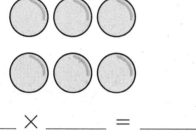

_____ × _____ = _____

_____ in all

2. How many in all? Multiply.

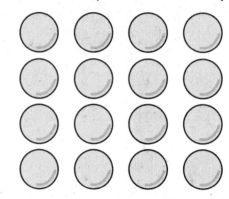

_____ × _____ = _____

_____ in all

 Draw a picture to solve. Use a separate sheet of paper.

3. Kayla places the cards in 5 rows. Each row has 2 cards. How many cards are there in all?

_____ × _____ = _____

_____ cards in all

4. Ms. Maya puts the chairs in rows. She makes 3 rows. She puts 6 chairs in each row. How many chairs does she use?

_____ × _____ = _____

_____ chairs in all

 **Draw a picture to solve. Use a separate sheet of paper.**

5. Maggie sets up her red checkers. She places 4 checkers in 3 of the rows on the board. How many checkers does she use?

_____ checkers

6. Pat makes a design on grid paper. He colors 4 rows. Each row has 5 squares. How many squares does he color?

_____ squares

© Macmillan/McGraw-Hill.

Repeated Subtraction and Division

 Solve. Draw a picture if you need help.

1. There are 9 boxes. Each car can carry 3 boxes. How many cars do you need?

$9 \div 3 =$ _____

_____ cars

2. There are 10 bags. Each van can hold 5 bags. How many vans do you need?

$10 \div 5 =$ _____

_____ vans

 Solve.

3. Nick has 12 beans. He subtracts groups of 6. How many equal groups of 6 can he make?

$12 \div 6 =$ _____

_____ groups

4. Jane has 15 eggs. She subtracts groups of 3. How many equal groups of 3 does she make?

$15 \div 3 =$ _____

 **Solve.**

5. Casey digs up 6 worms. She puts each pair of worms in a jar. How many jars does Casey need?

_____ jars

6. Mark has 20 rocks. He sorts them by size and puts them in groups of 5. He puts each group in a box. How many boxes does Mark use?

_____ boxes

Draw a picture to solve. Use a separate sheet of paper.

1. There are 8 bees on bushes. They are in 2 equal groups. How many bees are in each group?

$8 \div 2 =$ _____

_____ bees

2. There are 15 bugs on the ground. They are in 5 equal groups. How many bugs in each group?

$15 \div 5 =$ _____

_____ bugs

 Solve.

3. Rob has 10 seeds. He puts them into 2 equal groups. How many seeds are in each group?

$10 \div 2 =$ _____

_____ seeds

4. Riley has 12 bulbs. She divides them into 3 equal groups. How many bulbs are in each group?

$12 \div 3 =$ _____

_____ bulbs

 **Solve.**

5. Four friends want to share equally the 8 flowers they picked. How many flowers will each friend get?

_____ flowers

6. Ms. Paul has 18 flowers to plant. She divides the flowers into 6 equal groups. How many flowers are in each group?

_____ flowers

Problem Solving: Strategy
Use a Pattern

 Complete the table to solve.

1. How many wheels on 5 bicycles?

Number of bicycles	1	2	3	4	5
Number of wheels	2				

_____ wheels

2. How many wheels on 5 cars?

Number of cars	1	2	3	4	5
Number of wheels	4				

_____ wheels

 **Draw to solve. Use a separate sheet of paper.**

3. A spider has 8 legs. How many legs do 2 spiders have all together?

_____ legs

How many legs do 3 spiders have all together?

_____ legs

4. A ladybug has 6 legs. How many legs do 2 ladybugs have all together?

_____ legs

How many legs do 3 ladybugs have all together?

_____ legs

Make a table to solve. Use a separate sheet of paper.

5. A butterfly has 6 legs. How many legs are on 4 butterflies?

_____ legs

6. An octopus has 8 arms. How many arms are on 4 octopuses?

_____ arms